# Trillion Dollar

Women

# Trillion Dollar *Women*

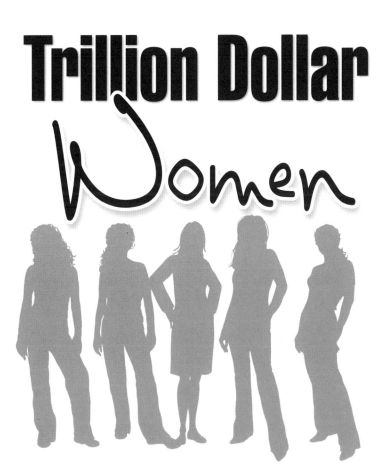

# Use Your Power
## to Make Buying & Remodeling Decisions

Tara-Nicholle Nelson, Esq.

**BuilderBooks.com**®
BOOKS THAT BUILD YOUR BUSINESS

*A Service of*
**NAHB**
NATIONAL ASSOCIATION
OF HOME BUILDERS

## Trillion Dollar Women: Use Your Power to Make Buying & Remodeling Decisions

BuilderBooks, a Service of the National Association of Home Builders

| | |
|---|---|
| Courtenay S. Brown | Director, Book Publishing |
| Doris M. Tennyson | Senior Editor |
| Natalie C. Holmes | Book Editor |
| Torrie L. Singletary | Production Editor |
| Manuel Garzon | Cover Design |
| Circle Graphics | Composition |
| Goodway Graphics | Printing |
| | |
| Gerald M. Howard | NAHB Executive Vice President and CEO |
| Mark Pursell | NAHB Senior Staff Vice President, Marketing & Sales Group |
| Lakisha Campbell | NAHB Staff Vice President, Publications & Affinity Programs |

### Disclaimer

This publication provides accurate information on the subject matter covered. The publisher is selling it with the understanding that the publisher is not providing legal, accounting, or other professional service. If you need legal advice or other expert assistance, obtain the services of a qualified professional experienced in the subject matter involved. Reference herein to any specific commercial products, process, or service by trade name, trademark, manufacturer, or otherwise does not necessarily constitute or imply its endorsement, recommendation, or favored status by the National Association of Home Builders. The views and opinions of the author expressed in this publication do not necessarily state or reflect those of the National Association of Home Builders, and they shall not be used to advertise or endorse a product.

Printed in the United States of America

11  10  09  08    1  2  3  4  5

ISBN-13: 978-0-86718-634-5
ISBN-10: 0-86718-634-8

Library of Congress Cataloging-in-Publication Data

Nelson, Tara-Nicholle.
  Trillion dollar women : use your power to making buying & remodeling
decisions / Tara-Nicholle Nelson.
     p. cm.
  Includes index.
  ISBN 978-0-86718-634-5
1. House buying. 2. Dwellings—Maintenance and repair—Decision
making. 3. Dwellings—Remodeling—Decision making. 4. Women
consumers. 5. Single women. I. Title.

  HD1379.N39 2008
  643'.12082—dc22

2007041392

For further information, please contact:

National Association of Home Builders
1201 15th Street, NW
Washington, DC 20005-2800
800-223-2665
Visit us online at www.BuilderBooks.com.

# Contents

## Appendixes

# Foreword

As a home builder, I can certainly attest to the fact that women's roles, responsibilities, and resources will continue to evolve in the years to come. Savvy home builders and general contractors recognize what this means to the residential construction industry. These builders and contractors welcome the opportunity to work with informed buyers. After all, as home builders, our ultimate goal is to create a home that meets the buyer's needs and exceeds their expectations.

There was a time when a woman accompanied her spouse to view a model home while her husband negotiated the price with the builder. She would assess the size of the kitchen, check the swing on the cabinet doors, and make sure she had a direct line of sight from the kitchen to the family room where she could watch her children at play.

Today women are leading the charge in home buying and remodeling decisions. In many cases, single women are heads of the household, and they have the economic power and wherewithal to buy or recreate the home of their dreams. Simply stated—I am excited about this new trend.

With this book, Tara-Nicholle Nelson has laid the foundation for a successful and enjoyable home buying or remodeling project. As a woman, she understands that the purchase or remodel of a home is something that a woman approaches from a psychological standpoint: How will this home make my life easier? Tara provides you, the reader, with the tools you need to identify and clarify your needs, communicate those needs to the builder or general contractor, and to ultimately produce the home of your dreams.

I encourage the reader to seek professionals who are clearly willing to work with you, listen to you, and be available to you throughout the duration of your new home construction or remodel project. My residential construction business is successful because I understand and appreciate the value of successful communication. In fact, my business philosophy is based on listening to the home buyer's concerns to gain a solid understanding of their issues and identify solutions that satisfy their unique housing needs.

NAHB has long been the voice of the housing industry, and BuilderBooks has been a resource for our members. Now with the publication of its first truly consumer-oriented book, *Trillion Dollar Women: Use Your Power to Make Buying & Remodeling Decisions,* BuilderBooks will also be a resource for you, the consumer.

**Sandy J. Dunn,**
2008 PRESIDENT-ELECT
NATIONAL ASSOCIATION OF HOME BUILDERS (NAHB)
AND PRESIDENT, B.J. BUILDERS, INC.

*NAHB is a Washington, D.C.-based trade association whose mission is to enhance the climate for housing and the building industry. Chief among NAHB's goals is providing and expanding opportunities for all consumers to have safe, decent and affordable housing. As "the voice of America's housing industry," NAHB helps promote policies that will keep housing a national priority. Founded in 1942, NAHB is a federation of more than 800 state and local associations. About one-third of NAHB's 235,000 members are home builders and/or remodelers. The remaining members are associates working in closely related fields within the housing industry, such as mortgage finance and building products and services.*

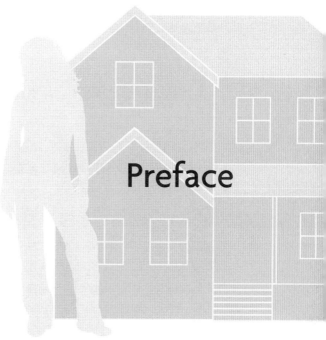

# Preface

My company's brand is called {RE} Think Real Estate. The idea of rethinking real estate arose from my conversations with women all over the country, who revealed that they loved the idea of the newly built or remodeled house but dreaded the process itself.

As Founder and Chief Visionary of {RE} Think Real Estate, my purpose is to marry my insider knowledge of real estate matters, including buying new construction and remodeling, with my understanding of women and their thought processes to create knowledge systems that literally transform women's real estate experiences—from home buying to home building to remodeling to even investing.

I wrote this book to help women overcome their fears and limiting thinking about home building and remodeling and to create an opportunity for women to evolve into educated, confident consumers.

It is my belief that women who experience real estate in this manner tend to move past their transaction or project and use the newly acquired boldness and control that they developed for their real estate projects in many other areas of their lives.

We've all heard the term, and we've probably all used it as well. But, what exactly is the *power of the purse*? It has been defined by various sources as follows:

"The constitutional power given Congress to raise and
spend money."                                —C-SPAN Congressional Glossary

"The influence that legislatures have over public policy
because of their power to vote money for public purposes.
The United States Congress must authorize the president's
budget requests to fund agencies and programs of the execu-
tive branch."
                —The New Dictionary of Cultural Literacy, Third Edition

"The ability of one group to manipulate and control the
actions of another group by withholding funding, or putting
stipulations on the use of funds."                —Wikipedia

"The collective purchasing power of American women who
are the primary decision makers in home construction and
remodeling projects, to the tune of hundreds of trillions of
dollars annually, especially when wielded boldly and successfully, with clarity, knowledge, and wisdom."
                —Tara-Nicholle Nelson

Let's assume the last definition is correct for our purposes. It begs
the question, who exactly are these women who are doling out all of
these dollars? These ladies (yourself included, perhaps) are the women
for whom this book was written. They are *Trillion Dollar Women*.

# Acknowledgments

I'd like to thank my husband, John Nelson; my sons, Roy and Clayton; and BuilderBooks visionaries Lakisha Campbell, Courtenay Brown, and Patricia Potts.

BuilderBooks would like to thank the following members of the NAHB Women's Council for their insight and guidance in the development of this publication: Karen Dry, president, Garrett Interiors, Inc.; Nicole Goolsby, president, Rion Homes, Inc.; Michelle A. Roberts, principal, Chatham Hill Residential Design and Build, LLC; Joanne (Jo) Theunissen, president, Howling Hammer Builders, Inc.; and Diane Willenbring, vice president, Willenbring Construction Incorporated.

# About the Author

Tara-Nicholle Nelson, MA, Esq., is a real estate broker and an accredited buyer's representative. Tara's real estate expertise is providing real estate education and services to niche markets, including single women, investors, and parties involved in legally complex transactions. As a single, teenage mother living in the Central California Valley, Tara completed Bachelor's and Master's degrees in Psychology at the California State University.

In 1998, Tara transformed her life. She lost 60 lb., left her abusive husband, moved her sons to the Bay Area, and enrolled in the prestigious University of California, Berkeley School of Law (Boalt Hall).

Immediately after graduating from law school in 2001, Tara, now a 25-year-old single mom of two boys, bought her first home in the Bay Area. After leaving a diverse law practice ranging from legal malpractice defense to corporate and real estate law, she began a unique real estate sales practice.

Realizing that several demographic groups—single women, seniors, investors, and bilingual clients—were being underserved, Tara melded insights from her psychology background, legal and negotiating savvy, and real estate expertise to innovate a system that she has now used to coach hundreds of single women and investors to success at the endeavor of purchasing a home. Today, Tara's passion is taking her system to women nationwide with {RE} Think Real Estate, a brand of educational resources designed to transform women's experience of real estate, and to inspire them to enhance their lives with property ownership.

# CHAPTER 1

# Who is the Trillion Dollar Woman?

Remember Lee Majors, the all-powerful, unstoppable *Six Million Dollar Man?* He was the government's most-prized secret agent for two reasons: (1) his body cost the government six million dollars to surgically repair, so he was literally worth millions to them (especially in the 1970s—imagine what Lee Majors would be worth today); and (2) he had bionic organs, arms, and legs, so his strength, speed, and vision far exceeded normal human ranges. Not to mention, he used his superhuman powers to further the interests of good and combat evil.

Increasingly, women consumers are to the residential construction industry what the *Six Million Dollar Man* was to the government—precious and valued. Why? I'd love to say it's because of our scintillating personalities or fun-loving spirits, but this is business. Like Lee Majors, women are precious and valuable to home builders and remodelers because their decisions are worth so much. However, I'm not talking a mere six million dollars, or even a billion dollars, but literally trillions of dollars in home building and remodeling transactions are controlled by female decision makers.

## The True Power of the Purse

According to a 2006 Joint Center for Housing Studies Harvard University study, *Buying for Themselves: An Analysis of Unmarried Female Home Buyers,* single women are buying homes at an incredible rate. In fact, 22% of homes sold in 2004 were sold to single women (Price tag: $550 billion), versus only 9% to single men. These numbers spike even higher for condos and townhomes, 30% of which are bought by single women.

But here's the real kicker—9 times out of 10, even in transactions where a single (unmarried) woman is not the home buyer, a single (individual) woman is the primary breadwinner and/or decision maker when it comes to building or remodeling decisions. Get a load of these mind-blowing numbers:

- Women make or direct 91% of home buying decisions. (Price tag: about $2 trillion)
- Women make 75% of the decisions about new homes. (Price tag: at least $250 billion)
- Women initiate 80% of all home improvement purchasing decisions, especially when it comes to big ticket orders such as kitchen cabinets, flooring, and bathroom overhauls.
- Women represent 51% of consumers that usually hire professionals for home improvement and remodeling projects. (Price tag: at least $100 billion)
- Women purchase 94% of home furnishings.

This data is not simply indicative of women spending their husbands' money. The vastness of these women-as-decision-maker numbers reflects an aggregation of three groups of some non-wage-earning women making purchasing decisions for their households with much larger numbers of (a) single women spending money that is all their own, (b) working, married women, and (c) stay-at-home moms who are the primary purchasing agents and decision makers in their households. Increasingly, even married women are bringing home more than their share of the bacon. In fact, according to the AFL-CIO's 2004 *Ask a Working Woman Survey* most working women contribute half or more of their household's income.

Virtually all of this data came out between 2004 and 2006. The male-dominated residential construction industry is taking notice of the fact that its most valuable customer—in terms of who decides where and how the housing and remodeling dollars are spent—is not the stereotypical male head of household, but rather, it is his single sister, his widowed mother, or even his wife! David Walentas, a Brooklyn, New York-based condominium developer, was surprised when he sold a third of his building's units to single women—$30 million worth of units, compared with the meager $19 million purchased by single men and $45 million sold to married couples. But what really stunned Walentas was the discovery of how many married women were writing the $60,000–$100,000 deposit checks.

> "It's the woman's check. It's not like a dual account—Joe and Suzy. It's just Suzy. I'm amazed."
>
> DAVID WALENTAS, DEVELOPER

So, you see, the term *power of the purse* has never been more appropriate. If I applied a corporate structure to the household, women would be the purchasing agent (and sometimes also the CEO and/or the sole proprietor). This truth is not limited to the realm of real estate, construction, or home remodeling. According to The Business and Professional Women's Foundation, in 2001 it was estimated that American women's collective purchasing power constituted the third largest market in the world, with a collective buying power exceeding the entire economy of Japan.

Clearly, every woman wields the power of the purse to a greater or lesser extent in every area of her life. But it takes more than just being a woman who spends money to be a trillion dollar woman. A true trillion dollar woman is one who

- knows her power, but wants to wield it wisely, for the good of her lifestyle and that of her family or housemates;
- knows the difference between delegation (assigning tasks to others skilled at those tasks, but retaining responsibility for their direction and supervision) and abdication (completely relinquishing all responsibility to someone else), and chooses to delegate, not abdicate, her construction and remodeling

projects to skilled builders and contractors (according to a 2005 Lowe's study, 40% list the kitchen as the space where they would hire a contractor, compared to 32% who would use a professional for the bathroom);

■ takes and retains ultimate responsibility for the success of her project;

■ knows that knowledge is power, and the root of the wise decision making she'll need to do to pull off a successful project, exercise her power wisely, and delegate without being taken advantage of; and, accordingly;

■ makes superhuman efforts to gain this knowledge.

Okay, so maybe superhuman efforts is an overstatement. But the trillion dollar woman does put some effort into educating herself before she takes on a home building or remodeling project. Like you, she researches her options, examines her lifestyle needs, and learns about the process by, for example, reading books like this one!

## QUIZ  So, are you a trillion dollar woman?

| | | | |
|---|---|---|---|
| 1. | You spend your free time visiting model homes—even when you're not in the market for a house. | True | False |
| 2. | Two out of three of your favorite television shows are HGTV shows. | True | False |
| 3. | You prefer *Architectural Digest* to *Vanity Fair*. | True | False |
| 4. | Your one-named heroes include Oprah, Ty, and Nate. | True | False |
| 5. | You think do-it-yourself is great for small projects, but outsourcing is the way to go when it's time to build or remodel your home. | True | False |
| 6. | You are in the market to purchase a new home or are thinking about remodeling an existing home. | True | False |
| 7. | You want information that will help execute your project with ease and success. | True | False |

If you answered true to at least five of the questions, congratulations—you are a trillion dollar woman, and this book was written just for you.

## Decisions, Decisions, Decisions: New Home or Existing Home?

The first stop along the path to building a new home is to decide whether to buy a new home or an existing (or resale) home. There are definitely "new home" trillion dollar women and "old house" trillion dollar women, but unless you identify strongly as one or the other, you have several factors to consider.

Buying new vs. existing: pros, cons, and other stuff to consider

| New Homes | Existing (Resale) Homes |
|---|---|
| You can choose your lot, location, décor, floor plan, and exterior design | You inherit the lot, location, décor, floor plan, and exterior design, but can customize it later at your expense |
| New, modern, shiny, bright, clean, and never lived in | Older, may have charming features of former eras of construction, lived in |
| Likely located in a new neighborhood or subdivision, without mature landscaping and sometimes with special taxes for emergency services and schools | Established neighborhoods feature established character, schools with proven track records, and mature landscaping |
| Neighborhoods are often located further distance from city center, jobs, causing a greater commute expense | Some established neighborhoods will be nearer to city center and workplaces |
| Typically more energy efficient, due to technological advances in insulation, appliances, and climate control systems, resulting in lower utility bills | Older homes may have drafts, leaks and old heating and cooling systems |
| 10-year builder warranty (on average, specifics depend on builder and state) included in purchase price | No real warranty included in price, but a home warranty can be purchased for about $300/year |

*(continued)*

**Buying new vs. existing: pros, cons, and other stuff to consider (*continued*)**

| New Homes | Existing (Resale) Homes |
|---|---|
| Lot sizes are typically smaller (single family residences) | Lot sizes are typically larger (single family residences) |
| Landscaping may not be included in purchase price | Landscaping is generally already installed and may be mature |
| Maintenance costs should be lower, as everything is new | Maintenance costs depend on maintenance history, age of home, and age of components |
| Modern construction techniques feature advances in fire and electrical safety, and resistance to natural hazards | Depending on age, may (or may not) feature the solid construction and old-growth materials used in old-world craftsmanship |
| Must wait until construction is complete to move in | Immediate move in (usually) |
| Planned communities may have restrictions on parking, landscaping, and exterior paint color selection | Every resident in your neighborhood can paint their home whatever color they want (good or bad) and park anywhere it is legal |
| Home has not settled, so problems may occur in coming years | Home has already settled, so problems may be easier to detect |

After considering the pros and cons, if you still can't decide between new and resale, you might need to consider an in-between option that will allow you to have the best of both worlds.

Even with all these considerations, you may not have a clear decision on whether your next home should be new or resale. Many women start the process by looking at both existing home and new home communities and develop a clear preference as their house hunt progresses. Remember, your ultimate goal is not just to pick new versus existing, but to acquire a home that makes life better for you and your family.

## Setting Your Building or Remodeling Project Up for Success: It's All in Your Head

Although Legos and Erector sets might not be as popular as Barbie and Bratz dolls among little girls, as a species women are highly inclined

## The best of both worlds: new and existing homes

| If you want . . . | But you also want . . . | You might consider . . . |
|---|---|---|
| A new home | To move in immediately, and you don't need to pick every tile or paint color yourself | An immediate delivery home. Builders/developers often construct a few unsold homes to finish out a mostly sold subdivision or to serve as model homes |
| A new home | A larger than usual lot, a completely unique home, a home in an older neighborhood, or one that has very unusual custom features (e.g., a mother-in-law cottage) | Building a custom home as opposed to a production home |
| A charming older home in an established neighborhood with mature landscaping or in a highly ranked school district | A modern kitchen and bathrooms, energy efficient home systems, and a large lot or other custom features | Buying and remodeling an existing home |

toward creation and transformation. How else could we explain our penchant for giving birth and watching TLC's *Trading Spaces*, despite the pain involved in both experiences?

For us, perhaps the purest opportunities to create and transform arise during home building and remodeling. Unfortunately, with all the other stuff on our plates—our careers and businesses, parenting responsibilities, managing our wellness and relationships, and all that stinking hair removal—the process of building or remodeling itself can seem less than fun and more like a drawn-out, tedious process, a necessary evil on the road to the golden grail of your dream home. A road seemingly riddled with bandits, speed bumps, and potholes at that!

As an industry insider, I'll be the very last to suggest that the dangers of unscrupulous builders, slimy salespeople, and construction defects are all in your head. But as a real estate broker and attorney who has coached thousands of women into their dream homes, I can tell you that a successful home building or remodeling experience is all in your head. That's where it starts, anyway. Let me explain.

## Defining Success

For many of our intrepid foremothers who braved the wilds of building or remodeling before this book was written, success at the endeavor started out defined as their vision made manifest—their fantasy of granite counters and Jacuzzi tubs converted into gleaming, tangible reality. Six months later, many of these ladies' definitions of success had gradually devolved into, well, simple completion.

Workers gone + running water + no more dumpsters = success

I'd like to elevate the concept of a successful building or remodeling project. I submit that the end result of a successful build or remodel is

- a home that makes your life easier and more beautiful,
- in ways that matter to you and your family, and
- culminates a building or remodeling process during which you felt respected, educated, and powerful.

Sound good? Let me tell you how to achieve it. As you read (and work) through this book, you'll be setting yourself up for success as you add layer upon layer of powerful knowledge, ultimately building a structure that mirrors that of a home (a one-room cabin, really, but you get the idea):

### Pour the foundation: your mindset

By mindset I don't mean just a can-do attitude; rah! rah! rah!; you go girl!; that sort of thing. I'm talking about a clear understanding of what it takes to get your project completed successfully. You should be clear about your wants, needs, priorities, lifestyle (current and future), resources, and options. Building or remodeling a home is a rare opportunity for you to create a house like no other home that exists on the planet—one that is designed specifically to suit the needs of you and your loved ones. A tailor can't work without measurements; likewise, you can't tailor a custom environment for your life without being clear about your wants and needs.

### Erect the four walls: the process, people, money, and design

After you've poured your foundation, the next step is to construct a framework of knowledge about

- **Process.** The steps you'll need to take on your path to building a new home or remodeling an existing home and what you can expect, sequentially (this information is targeted at helping you prepare in advance, preventing surprises and, thus, saving sanity).
- **People.** You need to understand the roles of the professionals with whom you'll interface through your build or remodel, from sales representatives to contractors to governmental permit authorities. You need to know what they do, who pays them to do it, and how to effectively manage and work with them to get it done.
- **Money.** There are various sources, types, and considerations involved in securing financing for your construction project. You need to understand how to select financing that makes sense for your personality and your family's finances and how to create and manage your project budget.
- **Design.** There are specific features and strategies you can use to explosively maximize the lifestyle-enhancing potential of your project, as well as design features and issues that matter to lots of trillion dollar women, including things you need to know about remodeling or building within a condo, townhome, or co-op unit and how to make your couture home eco-chic, using environmentally responsible strategies and materials.

### Pitch the roof: knowledge-powered confidence

By this I don't mean a "get-out-of-my-way-and-hand-me-a-hammer-so-I-can-build-this-house-myself" sort of confidence. Nor do I mean that fake, blustery, know-it-all bravado some people feel the need to put on when they deal with salespeople, which gets none of your questions answered and is very transparent, to boot! Nope—I'm talking about the calm, assured, mature confidence of a woman who knows

- that it's perfectly okay to ask questions;
- which questions to ask and how to interpret and apply the answers;
- how to express herself in the vocabulary of the pros she's working with;
- when and how to effectively, respectfully express when something isn't working, in a way that earns her respect; and
- things that should and shouldn't be deal-maker or deal-breaker.

Simply laying the roof on top of this house of knowledge by working through this book isn't the end of your journey of preparing for a successful home build or remodel the trillion dollar woman way. There are two additional books that every trillion dollar woman should study before their build or remodel project and reference during the process.

I recently authored *The Savvy Woman's Homebuying Handbook: 150 Insider Secrets, Decision-Making Guides and Online Resources, Plus the ONE Action Plan You Need* (Prosperity Way Press, 2007). This book goes even deeper into the mindset management tools and strategies that facilitate the transition from procrastinating would-be home buyer to home owner; delves into the basics of money, mortgages, and matching a mortgage with your lifestyle needs; and explores the intricacies of a home buying transaction step by step, including detailed tutorials on contracts, negotiations, escrow and closing, and even asset protection strategies. Throughout the book, the true stories of my real-life savvy women home buyer clients add some hilarity to the morality tales they underscore. This book is a must for trillion dollar women who are buying a new home from a builder or developer or buying an existing home that they plan to remodel.

The second must-have book is *Building Your Home: An Insider's Guide, Second Edition* by Carol Smith (BuilderBooks.com®, 2005). *Building Your Home* drills down into the individual steps and phases of the home building process at an incredible level of detail. This book provides a potent dose of how-to for the complex endeavor of home building above and beyond the primer provided in this book, from deciding to build, to selecting your builder and your site, to creating your plan, to the actual sequence in which your home will be built and beyond! *Building Your Home* is conducive for use as your nuts-and-bolts reference during the entire process of, well, building your home!

This book, in contrast to the others, focuses on providing knowledge to feed the informational cravings specific to smart women who are in the position to make or influence building or remodeling decisions. Additionally, it redefines the concept of what a successful home build or remodel is—as we've already discussed—and provides mindset and decision-making tools to help transform your experience of the project from a tedious task to a rare opportunity to enhance your lifestyle on an incredible scale. In accordance with my mantra of lifestyle enhancement, this book presents a number of specific strategies, design considerations, and features and amenities for your new (or newly remodeled) home that will make your life easier, and your home more beautiful, efficient, and environmentally responsible—all things that are important to trillion dollar women, yourself included.

## Why a Book Just for Women?

My life's work arises out of the essential truth that women simply think about, shop for, and make major decisions about their homes differently than men. And because women comprise such a huge chunk of the real decision makers when it comes to building and remodeling homes, I felt that the trillion dollar woman deserved a new home building and remodeling survival guide of her own. One that is custom tailored to her thought and decision-making processes, providing knowledge organized in the same way her brain works through the issues which arise while having a new home built or having an existing home remodeled, and specifically answering the specific concerns many women express.

A detailed how-to guide is critical to success, but it's not enough for the trillion dollar woman. Beyond how-to, she also craves a book

## Trillion Dollar Tip #1

### Home couture: custom or production?

In fashion, *haute couture* refers to the creation of exclusive, custom-fitted clothes of expensive fabrics. *Haute couture* is always made to order for a specific customer.

Similarly, custom homes are built to order from a unique design created specifically for a particular home buyer. Custom home builders tend to specialize in the construction of homes that are almost always luxury or high-end single-family homes, which are built on lots that belong to the home buyer. In urban or established neighborhoods, individuals desiring custom homes must often purchase an older home on a desirable lot, level it, and have a new home built on the site.

Production homes, however, comprise the vast majority of new homes that are built and purchased nationwide. Often referred to as tract homes, homes in subdivisions, or semi-customs, production homes are generally constructed by builders/developers who own the lots they build on. Production home communities normally offer a number of standard building plans, exterior looks (or elevations), and upgrade options. Production homes can be condos, townhomes, or single-family homes that range from inexpensive entry-level homes to high-end luxury homes.

Most of the information in this book is tailored for trillion dollar women who are buying production homes. The trillion dollar woman who wants to build a custom home should also read *Building Your Home: An Insider's Guide, Second Edition.*

that will tell her what to expect—this is absolutely the most effective freak-out prevention strategy, and before she gets to either how-to or what to expect, mindset management is a critical first step. Mindset management deals with how you think about this project and the role it plays in your life. Mindset management is about paradigms and perspectives, not nails and sheet rock.

This book has a number of additional features, which are driven by the results of my research into the neuropsychology underlying how women think through their home building and remodeling decisions:

### Unbiased and not driven by a commission

According to a 2004 Sears Roebuck and Company *Her Home* survey, 94% of women are concerned about getting a fair price from construction professionals. Women also believe that good home repair professionals are harder to find than good doctors, financial planners, or real estate agents. You can rest assured that the information in this book is not motivated by a commission. My goal in writing this book is to educate you. I'm not trying to sell you anything!

### Advisory

Women may be closing the wage gap, but the information gap is steadily widening. Many women are still at an informational disadvantage when it comes to understanding construction basics. (What is that about, anyway? Does every guy spend a summer working in construction during college or something? Or do they teach it in boys' gym class on rainy days? I digress...) This information gap causes many women to approach their projects warily and with a lot of concern that they might be taken advantage of by builders, salespeople, contractors, etc. The *Her Home* survey found that 63% of women believed they were charged more than men for the same work. The survey also found that 3 out of 5 women home owners said they'd rather get an hour of free advice from Bob Vila than from Dr. Phil. Accordingly, the knowledge solutions in this book are organized from the perspective of your personal advisor on issues that repeatedly come up for trillion dollar women and to generate clarity and diminish fear, so that you can boldly manage your hired professionals—instead of them managing you!

### 360° perspective on life

Women don't think about a home in isolation from the rest of their life. Rather, women tend to take a very holistic view, considering how each and every feature or amenity or downside of a home will impact every other area of their lives. Therefore, I will treat the topic of your home as inextricably intertwined with the rest of your life and will highlight less-than-obvious implications of home specifics.

### Lifestyle enhancement

The goal of this entire home building or remodeling endeavor should be to make your life easier, better, and more beautiful. As the process unfolds, it will be easy to forget these overarching goals as you get bogged down in the minutiae of selecting tile and doing walkthroughs. My goal is to help keep you mindful of and accountable to your lifestyle enhancement aims as your building project moves toward the finish line!

The first step toward creating this momentum in your new home purchase or remodeling project and in your life is mindset management. Let's get started!

# Mindset and Lifestyle
## Getting Things in Motion and Keeping Them on Track

In the residential construction industry, soft costs are those expenses that are associated with the things you need to build or remodel your home, but are not hard costs such as lumber, plumbing, tile, and appliances. Usually soft costs are things you need to put in place before you get started in order for your project to run smoothly.

As you embark upon the process of building or remodeling your home the trillion dollar woman way, your two most critical soft costs are your mindset and lifestyle. In order to have a fearless and joyful building or remodeling experience, you'll need to manage your mindset and be clear about your lifestyle aims for the project before you get started with the nuts and bolts of construction.

So, how do you manage your mindset? To effectively manage your mindset, you will need to take the following steps toward mental readiness:

1. Identify mental obstacles, fears, and limiting thinking
2. Shatter fears with information
3. Shift into an empowered mindset

There are three essential elements for clarifying your lifestyle for a successful build or remodel: (1) your vision and values that impact your home life, (2) your priorities, and (3) your plans and timelines (for the next few phases of your life). The goal is to achieve clarity on all three elements.

So as you can see, a determined mind and a clear vision for your current and future lifestyle are the building blocks for the entire project. Effective management of these soft costs will allow you to

- create the spark that gets you started,
- provide direction for the hundreds of decisions that you will be asked to make, and
- facilitate course correction if and when things start to veer track.

To skip this step in the process would be like driving your car down the street without defogging the window first—a setup for failure!

## Managing Your Mindset

This book will give you literally thousands of things to think about; but first, let's consider how you think about things. I strongly believe that the way you think about things (your mindset) is actually more important than what you think about (the actual information or data). Mindset is simply more powerful because energy follows thought. If you don't think you can do something, even if you have the ability to do it—you won't; but when you think you can do something, even if it seems impossible—you will.

### Inside the Minds of Trillion Dollar Women

In speaking to trillion dollar women (and trillion dollar women-to-be) all over America, I've realized that there are legions of "stalled" trillion dollar women out there. These women so dread the process of building and remodeling, that they avoid it altogether. Despite having the resources and desire to live in a new or remodeled home, they choose to live in homes that are dysfunctional for their lifestyles because they *think* they are too fearful, uncertain, or overwhelmed to proceed.

In my conversations with these women, I've discovered that there are some fairly consistent messages they give themselves to justify their fear of the building or remodeling process. Do you regularly recite any of these fearful expressions?

## Fearful expressions of stalled trillion dollar women

*I'm so overwhelmed already! With my kids, my job, and taking care of myself, when am I supposed to find the time to build a house or supervise a contractor?*

*I can't imagine coming home to all that mess every day while the work is being completed.*

*It's so expensive! I'm not made of money. I've owned my home for 10 years, and I'd like to stay in it, but it needs some major upgrades, and we need more room. Where on earth would I get that kind of money?*

*Builders are shady, and I don't know much about construction. I'd probably get ripped off if I tried to build or remodel my home.*

*Tract homes are so cookie-cutter. I love the idea of a new home, but it seems like I'd be living in a home exactly like everyone else's in my neighborhood.*

*It seems like new homes are built so much shoddier than old homes. The last thing I need in my life is a house that will fall apart as soon as I move in.*

*I would love to be able to customize my own home, and the new home neighborhoods in my town are really nice. But new homes in my area seem so much more expensive than old homes.*

*I'm single, and it seems like there are too many decisions that I don't know how to make. That's a big burden for me to take on by myself.*

*I'm just scared. I've been renting for so long that I don't even know where to start. But I know I'd like to buy new when I do buy.*

### I have good news . . .

If you have contemplated (or uttered) any of these fearful expressions, you are in good shape! All of these concerns and fears are resolvable. Take my word for it. Whether you decide to build or to remodel, it is very doable, and no matter which of the fearful expressions reflects your specific concerns, you will find information throughout this book to help you shatter that fear or navigate around a particular issue.

### . . . and bad news

If you believe these fearful expressions, you are a victim of your own limiting thinking. These expressions can render you incapable of achieving a goal that you clearly have the ability to achieve.

You must stop speaking and/or thinking negatively about yourself and about the building or remodeling process immediately. Your words and thoughts will ultimately manifest into your reality. The stalled trillion dollar woman who is obsessed with the prospect of getting ripped off inevitably ends up hiring the cheapest contractor—someone who was recommended by her brother-in-law's cousin who tends to "know people." She takes his advice and passes up dozens of more expensive, but more qualified builders. In the end, she gets ripped off. Or, she becomes so concerned about the expense of a new home that she ends up choosing every upgrade option ever created. She ends up driving the price of her once-affordable home up to astronomical levels, in a stunning, but common, display of self-fulfilling prophecy.

If you are the renter who tells yourself that you simply can't afford to buy new, or the home owner who just can't imagine where you'll find the money to remodel, that will be your reality. By repeatedly speaking and thinking negatively, you will literally hypnotize yourself into a state of immobility, and you will act accordingly. For example, you will not consciously attend to your personal finances to see where change could be made or investigate options for financing your new home or remodeling project, and ultimately your dreams will be as impossible as you imagine them to be.

## Shifting Into the Empowered Mindset of a Trillion Dollar Woman

To move into an empowered mindset, you must commit to the concept that you can and will create the home you desire, and start speaking your commitment into reality. Stop mentally wrangling over if you will be able to build or remodel your home, and start working through the questions of how and when your project will begin. To be a trillion dollar woman, you must act accordingly. You can begin to move toward your dream by taking the following steps:

### Look online—but not in person, yet

Take a virtual tour of local new home communities, and start educating yourself about the sort of home, neighborhood, and community amenities that are available. If you visit a model home without your real estate agent in tow, most builders will refuse to pay the real estate agent for you later.

### Cultivate clarity

Develop an image in your mind of how you would like your home life to be different and how that translates into things you'd like to change when you remodel your home.

### Raise your financial consciousness

Track your household spending and create a spending and savings plan that is aligned with your priorities, including a future remodel or new home.

### Practice conscious communication

Talk to a real estate or mortgage professional regarding the options for financing a construction project.

### Educate yourself

Read books like this one and others, search the Internet, and elevate your knowledge level, which in turns increases your ability to control the direction of your build or remodel project.

Online resources for developing the mindset of a trillion dollar woman

| Site Title | Site URL | Site Description |
| --- | --- | --- |
| National Association of Home Builders (NAHB) Consumer Resources | www.nahb.org | Guides you through every stage of home building, remodeling, and ownership |
| {RE}Think Real Estate | www.REThinkRealEstate.com | Provides the how-to, what-to-expect, and mindset management techniques for women who want to buy, sell, invest, or remodel homes |
| Conscious Bookkeeping | www.ConsciousBookkeeping.com | Offers telecourses and resources for financial therapy and managing your household finances consistently with what you value |
| The Secret | www.TheSecret.tv | Presents practical steps for creating and maintaining a mindset of abundance based on the Law of Attraction |
| Steve Pavlina's Blog | www.StevePavlina.com/blog | Lists a mindset mastery that you can use immediately |

## Clarifying Your Lifestyle

*Crystal clear*—I love that term. Its visual implication is so powerful. It implies that things are not just recently-cleaned-window clear, or minimally-smudged-eyeglass clear, but *crystal* clear; so clear that you can look at the issue from any side and see straight through to the other side.

As a trillion dollar woman, you need to be crystal clear about the end goal of your building or remodeling process. The Craftsman in the suburbs you want to build is not the end itself, but rather a means to an even higher, more important end. The remodeled bathroom, complete with steam shower and Jacuzzi tub, is also not the ultimate goal. What we all seek when we start a project like this is a better lifestyle. Better than the one we have now.

Better how? That part is up to you. It could be a lifestyle that is more convenient and comfortable, one that flows with more ease. Perhaps your idea of a better lifestyle is one that allows you and your family to do more of the things that you'd like to do. Maybe a better lifestyle to you is one that is friendlier to our planet than the one you currently live, or one that simply provides you more opportunities to experience beauty than your current lifestyle.

The bottom line is that your home is quite literally the environment in which your daily living activities—a huge part of your lifestyle—take place. Very rarely in your lifetime will you have the ability to impact the quality of your life as profoundly as you do when you build or remodel a home. If you do not focus on the fact that lifestyle enhancement is your overall goal, you can get swept into the "vortex of cuteness" (in the words of one of my favorite clients) and end up creating a home that may be a showplace, but is inconsistent with the way you live your life.

Fortunately, the process of developing clarity is actually fun! I've developed a few Lifestyle Clarity-Building Exercises to help you. These exercises are similar to *Cosmopolitan* magazine's ever-popular Cosmo quizzes, but more profound on a number of levels. (And I know a couple of women who have had some pretty profound insights after a Cosmo quiz!) These exercises will help you unearth some things about yourself that you may have never known. Many trillion dollar women find that they emerge from the lifestyle phase with new self-knowledge, new ideas, and a new excitement about their future. This is bigger than your home or your remodeling dreams—this is about your life, generally! With the information you will gain from these exercises, you'll be able to customize your entire building or remodeling experience, tailoring it and your home to the lifestyle you really want to create.

You should actually block out time in your calendar to get these exercises done. The documents you create will come in very handy as you make decisions during the building or remodeling project.

If you are building or remodeling with a spouse, significant other, or housemate, you should offer them the opportunity to complete these exercises, too. Share as much information as you feel comfortable sharing. The goal should be to make both of your lives better.

## Lifestyle Clarity-Building Exercise #1: Define Your Values and Priorities

Have you ever been watching *Cribs* or *Dream Home* and thought, "Wow, I guess it'd be nice to have a gold-plated, marble antique toilet or a 40-seat movie theater complete with ticket booth, but if I had that money to put into my house, I'd probably build a big playhouse for the kids, a gourmet kitchen, or a backyard cottage for my parents." I know I have!

This is an example of aligning your home with your values. We all have different values, and no one set of values is superior to another. What is important is that, in the final analysis, the home you live in is consistent with what you value—rather than being consistent with today's popular trends in home design or what the Johnsons have down the street. In order to make sure your newly built or remodeled home enhances your lifestyle and reflects your values, you must first get clarity on what it is you actually value.

The exercise of articulating your values starts with a brainstorming session on the misleadingly simple question, "What is truly important to me?" Schedule an hour of uninterrupted time, find a comfortable place, grab a bar of organic dark chocolate or your favorite coffee drink, and write the top 15-20 things that are truly important to you in the space that is provided on page 24. You may write words, phrases, or sentences. For example, "that my kids go to college," or "that I live a well and happy life," or "yoga."

Got your list? Good. Now abstract the things you wrote into one-word values, some of which may be the driving force behind four or five of your first responses. For example, wellness might be the value—the thing that is important to you—that is underlying four or five of the things you said were important to you on your first pass (such as yoga, healthy diet, good night's sleep, etc.). Other values which many trillion dollar women tend to hold include:

- beauty
- wellness
- family
- love
- success
- growth
- vitality
- connection

For an exhaustive list of over 350 values, visit: www.stevepavlina.com/articles/list-of-values.htm.

Once you have a list of values that you feel truly represent what is most important to you, rank them in order of importance. Then you'll be ready to move on to the next step in developing clarity as to the lifestyle you want to live in your newly built or remodeled home.

## Lifestyle Clarity-Building Exercise #2: Write the Vision

The next step in the process is to draft your Vision of Home statement, which should describe the desired state of your life after you build your home. It should encompass all elements of your life, including where, how, and how much you live, work, play, and rest, etc.

Before you've even started looking at developments or sketching out your dream post-remodel kitchen, you will have already made the emotional commitment to this project. The Vision of Home statement will help you maintain this commitment, through all the drudgery and detail work involved in getting into your home. The idea is to paint such a vivid picture of the life you want that it excites you to action and keeps your commitment, energy, and enthusiasm levels high—from start to finish.

Fully engaging in and completing this exercise will place you in an incredible position of power when it comes to communicating your

| What is truly important to me? | | |
|---|---|---|
| | Value | Rank |
| 1 | | |
| 2 | | |
| 3 | | |
| 4 | | |
| 5 | | |
| 6 | | |
| 7 | | |
| 8 | | |
| 9 | | |
| 10 | | |
| 11 | | |
| 12 | | |
| 13 | | |
| 14 | | |
| 15 | | |
| 16 | | |
| 17 | | |
| 18 | | |
| 19 | | |
| 20 | | |

needs and wants to your team of professionals and staying on track throughout your process. In fact, depending on how specific your Vision of Home statement is, you might be able to pull a subset of points from it to actually describe the master bedroom suite you want to your architect. A written Vision of Home will also help keep you accountable to yourself throughout—and long after—the process is over. Your Vision of Home can help you make decisions that are consistent with your lifestyle needs and preferences.

There are definitely elements that must be covered, but the form of your Vision of Home statement can be totally driven by your style; a one-page list of bullet points works for one trillion dollar woman, whereas another might want to journal an epic 10-page narrative. The point is—write it down.

To begin, think of your life as a little ecology, or pattern of interaction between an organism (you) and your environment (the people, places, and things that populate your life). Every element is inextricably intertwined with every other element. To get a visual, think of those middle school food chain charts—if one fungus in the remote reaches of the Himalayas dies off, the price of *Vanity Fair* magazine goes up through some intricate relationship involving the sun and herbivores in South America.

Similarly, if you tweak one element of your Vision of Home statement, the vision itself will change. For example, let's assume that right now you are single, with no kids, and you are able to support your lifestyle working as a freelance graphic designer. You have a vision of continuing this lifestyle. So that you don't have to go work for a firm, you might incorporate the following elements into your Vision of Home statement:

- *Generate X number of additional projects every month, and working the extra hours to complete them*
- *Keep mortgage payment under X number of dollars per month (vs. the Y number of dollars you could afford if you went to work for a firm)*
- *Buy a new townhome or condo vs. a single-family home*

- *Customize new home with CAT-5 wiring and extra outlets for computer equipment*
- *Live within a short distance from parents, friends, or favorite social haunts, so I don't have to spend a lot to visit*
- *Walk to yoga studio on Wednesday afternoons and drive a few minutes to Whole Foods to pick up lots of ready-to-eat stuff on the weekends*
- *Pull car into a secure garage after I get home from visiting my parents, the yoga studio, my book club . . .*

If you decided to work for a firm, you can imagine how things would change. Your preferred locations would be driven more by your workplace than your leisure activities. If you add children to the mix, things would shift again. You would need a bigger space (and income). You probably would have less time to walk to yoga, etc.

When you are crafting your Vision of Home statement you will need to think beyond the number of bedrooms and bathrooms and consider how your home will complement your lifestyle. To make sure that you do not finish this chapter without at least attempting to craft your statement, I want you to take a sip of your coffee or a bite of your organic chocolate bar and write a 3–5 sentence Vision of Home statement on page 27.

| My vision of home . . . |
| --- |
|  |
|  |
|  |
|  |
|  |
|  |
|  |
|  |
|  |
|  |
|  |
|  |
|  |
|  |
|  |

Now that you have an initial Vision of Home statement, I want you to go a step further and consider how your vision aligns with your ideal day. This step should help you gain an even deeper clarity in terms of your current or desired lifestyle.

## My ideal day . . .

Hour by hour, write exactly what you would do in your ideal day in your new home. For example what time would you get out of bed? What's the first thing you would do? What next? And so forth, until you go to bed.

By now you should have a written document that describes your vision of your life after your home is built or remodeled. Now go back to Exercise #1 and make sure that your vision is consistent with your values.

## Lifestyle Clarity-Building Exercise #3: Develop Your Life Plan Timeline

The purpose of this quick exercise is to ensure that no major predictable life events are overlooked in the process of planning your building or remodeling project. This is not to suggest that every event you list on your personal timeline must be provided for in your new (or newly remodeled) home. The point is to be conscious of all these items in your decision-making process. For example, you may not expand your current home to have as many bedrooms as you'll need for the eventual size of your family, but you will make this decision consciously and with plans to move after your first child reaches a certain age. Here is a partial list of events to include in your timeline:

- children: births, adoptions, school district considerations, going to college/moving out
- parents: moving in with you, moving into a separate home from them
- work: making partner, retiring, starting your own business, changing careers
- relationships: getting married (or divorced), moving in with a significant other, moving in with a housemate, or separating from a housemate

You will want to consider these events—all of which will have an impact on what you need and want in your home—in terms of how many years out from now you plan for them to take place.

| My life plan timeline | |
|---|---|
| Children | |
| Parents | |
| Work | |
| Relationships | |
| | |
| | |
| | |
| | |
| | |
| | |
| | |
| | |
| | |
| | |
| | |
| | |
| | |
| | |
| | |
| | |

## Ensuring a Soft and Smooth Process

With your newfound clarity on your values and priorities, your written Vision of Home statement, and personal timeline you are now in a position of power to

a. plan a home that furthers your values and allows you to live your vision; and,

b. hold yourself and your entire construction team accountable to your values and vision, as you proceed through this process.

When you hire the first member of your team, you can use these documents to clearly describe the home environment you want to create and make sure they can catch the vision.

I encourage you to use these documents throughout the process to ensure that the decisions you make are aligned with your desired lifestyle. Although mindset and lifestyle considerations are soft costs, they have the power to make your build or remodel run smoothly.

# CHAPTER 3

# Building Blocks

## The People and the Process of Buying a Newly Constructed Home

This chapter will help you build a framework for understanding the home building process, including the people involved and how the process will unfold. We'll be building this framework on top of the foundation you've just set:

- **A bold mindset.** You are fearless when it comes to asking and even demanding, if necessary, information when you become conscious of a gap in your knowledge.
- **Clarity on the lifestyle objectives of your home building process.** You can check in with your own vision, values, priorities, and life plans at each round of decision making to ensure that your decisions stay aligned with them.

Whether you are learning the Argentine tango or learning how to drive a stick shift, there are four basic phases to mastering a skill:

- **Phase 1: Unconscious incompetence.** You have no idea what you're doing, but you don't even know enough to care about your lack of knowledge.
- **Phase 2: Conscious incompetence.** You still don't know what you are doing, but you are very, sometimes painfully, aware of your lack of knowledge.

- **Phase 3: Conscious competence.** You understand the information, but working with it requires intense focus and attention and you are still aware of any gaps in your understanding.
- **Phase 4: Unconscious competence.** At this point, you have such mastery of the material that you are able to work with it and use it without even thinking.

Now, remember, we're building an edifice of information here; we're creating the structure of knowledge about building a new home that is necessary to build your home the trillion dollar woman way. However, we aren't really seeking total, unconscious competence-level mastery of this information, because (a) you have plenty of other things in your life that you really need to master in order to manage your family, your business, your career, and your life; and (b) you will be hiring folks who have mastered this stuff with years of experience and education—far beyond what is possible from reading a single book.

What we're shooting for here is Phase 3, a conscious competence about the home building process. So that you can converse with your team of professionals in their vocabulary, but you don't need to be able to swing the hammer yourself! Also, you want to be conscious of the things that you don't know and will need to ask.

There is one critical difference (okay, maybe more than one) between learning the tango and learning about the process of building your new home. When you are educating yourself about new home construction, there are some major decisions that you have to make along the way. (When you're learning the tango, the big decision is: ruffled dress or polka dots? But I digress.) So, as we build your knowledge base together, I'll give you some inside pointers and things to consider along the way.

Speaking of the process, let's drill down into the details so you will know how the process will unfold and who the players are.

## Buying New Construction: The People and The Process

Visualize the path to the door of your new home as a cobblestone path that meanders through a small village. At different points throughout the village, you will need to make decisions about which way to turn and how to proceed. To get home, you will need to interact with different villagers along the path—some of whom you will pay, and others who will give (well, lend) money to you. Still others will simply provide wisdom that they have developed by helping others to journey along the same decision-making path that you are now traveling. Other villagers will simply want to take your order and relay your decisions to the people who are actually building your home.

Your path may be windy or straight, short or long, depending on the decisions you make, the skill of the villagers you encounter, and the type of new construction you are purchasing. For example, you may have fewer choices to make if you are purchasing a condo or townhome as opposed to a semi-custom detached home.

It literally does take a small village of professionals to complete the process of purchasing a new-construction home. You will spend a great deal of time with many of them during certain phases of the home buying process. Therefore, it is important to develop a positive and pleasant interpersonal relationship with them. With others, their role as the gatekeeper to a particular community or builder that you want to buy from will trump the interpersonal issues. You'll work with them because you must, but it can optimize your interactions if you understand their role and motivations more fully.

Everyone in your new-home-buying village plays a specific purpose or role. To retain control of your transaction and know more precisely who to ask to do what, you first need to understand who these people are, what their roles are, who they work for, and how they get paid.

# The Village People

## Real Estate Agent

A good real estate agent is to your transaction what an attorney is to a lawsuit. As the client, you provide the overall direction and vision for the outcome, and they actually facilitate the transaction. Your agent's job is to

- help you determine your buying power and select a reputable mortgage provider and financing options that fit your vision and lifestyle
- help you decide whether to buy a new home or a resale home
- make you aware of communities that meet your needs and accompany you to view and evaluate properties
- provide expert knowledge and objective information about resale considerations and other factors impacting whether a property is right for your needs
- help you decide on a community, a lot, and a model of home that makes sense for you
- communicate and negotiate on your behalf with the builder/developer/seller
- demystify the contract and your obligations, as well as builder's obligations to you
- connect you with other professionals and resources before, during, and after your transaction, including resources in the fields of mortgage, escrow, financial planning, legal, and home maintenance

Your real estate agent is your advisor throughout this process. Their value to you lies largely in the fact that they are familiar with the local new home communities; they possess an insider's knowledge of local builders' reputations and incentives you might be able to receive; and that they can anticipate, avoid, and resolve glitches and propose solutions.

Your agent's role in your new home buying transaction can be more or less central depending on your builder's transaction flow. For example, some builders' sales representatives handle the paperwork that your real estate agent would ordinarily handle, such as drafting the contract and other items. However, it is your realtor's responsibility to make sure you fully understand and agree to everything before you sign anything.

Your real estate agent works for you. Although the builder's sales representatives will likely be real estate agents also, they are employed

## Trillion Dollar Tip #2

### Warning: do not enter the model home unaccompanied

It's tempting. I know! The model homes are calling your name—all over town. But here's the deal: What seems to you to be just a casual Sunday stroll through the sales office and into the models, just to look and see, can actually have a huge and detrimental impact on your home buying process.

Builders require real estate agents to accompany their clients on the first visit to their community. When you visit a community together, your agent registers as your representative and forever after you can visit as many times as you want, no problem. However, if you visit the sales office or the model home without your agent—even once, just for a few minutes—you will lose the benefit of the builder's offer to pay for your agent's commission. Effectively speaking, going to the model home by yourself for the first time means that you will lose the benefit of your agent's advice, representation, and advocacy during your transaction.

If you are just itching to see the model homes, shop the local new home communities online. Then, as soon as you find an agent, make an appointment to visit the new home communities you might even be remotely interested in, so that you can register with your agent on your first visit. Then, you can spend as many Sundays as you want strolling leisurely through the community—with or without your agent!

by the builder and they work for the builder, even though they are providing customer service to you. Unlike the builder's sales representatives, your real estate agent owes you legal and fiduciary duties of competence, confidentiality, and loyalty.

Many builders cooperate or *co-broke* with agents, meaning they pay your agent's commission for you. Real estate agents usually get paid commissions ranging from 2–3% of the purchase price of the home.

# Mortgage Professionals

A mortgage is a bank loan that provides the money to pay for the construction and/or ownership of your new home. A mortgage professional is your liaison with the bank, who helps you locate and secure the financing you need.

There are two types of mortgage professionals you can work with in financing your new home (and its construction): a bank's mortgage representative or a mortgage broker. Whichever one you work with, there is a small set of key duties they will perform:

- collect the personal data for all borrowers (yourself, your spouse, co-owners, etc.) including information on credit, income, work history, assets and other indicators of your ability to pay to determine your qualifications for a mortgage loan
- ask about your personality, lifestyle, and future plans to determine the ideal mortgage loan programs for you
- educate you about the considerations, implications, and pitfalls of available mortgage loan options and how these options will impact your life
- package your information and communicate it to the bank or banks for their consideration, before and during your home buying process

No matter which type of professional you choose, you should view their function as shopping around to find a mortgage with the best interest rates available based on your qualifications, and with repayment terms that suit your lifestyle, personality, and future plans. The key differences between the two professionals are who they work for and the universe of loan programs available to them to shop for you.

## Bank Mortgage Representatives

This mortgage professional works for a bank. They get paid a mixture of salary and commissions from the loans they close. You pay the commission in the form of an origination fee that is usually 1% of the loan amount.

Most often, if you are offered a mortgage through the builder/developer of your home, or if you are required by the builder to be preapproved by a particular mortgage lender in order to proceed with the sale, the mortgage professional your builder connects you with will be a bank's mortgage representative. (Some of the larger builders actually have their own internal mortgage banks that make mortgages to fund the construction and ownership of homes they build.) If your personal bank offers mortgages the mortgage consultant at the bank is also a mortgage representative.

Bank mortgage representatives are supposed to find you an ideal loan, but they typically only shop among the loans offered by the bank that employs them. (Some can broker outside loans, but only for very small amounts. Bank mortgage representatives will almost always seek to get your primary mortgage funds from their employer.) You might want to work with a bank's mortgage representative in the following instances.

### The builder offers substantial incentives for using their preferred or in-house lender

Most builders' primary concern is that the financing element of the transaction goes through. For this reason, they often offer major incentives to buyers who take their mortgage loan from a preferred or in-house lender. It is not uncommon for builders to offer price reductions, closing costs credit, home owner association dues payments, or upgrades and landscaping to buyers who work with the preferred or in-house lender. If the incentives are desirable and substantial, and the mortgage offered by the preferred lender is competitive, it's a no-brainer that you would want to work with the preferred bank's mortgage representative.

### You are an A+ borrower or the bank's target customer

If you have great credit, strong income, a stable work history, and plenty of assets, you will most often get great rates and loan repayment terms at a large national bank. Also, if the bank offers a unique mortgage loan that you are an ideal candidate for, or if the bank has a corporate mandate to lend to a specific type of borrower, which you are, you are also likely to get good rates and terms. For example, many credit unions are supposed to lend to members of a certain profession, like teachers, nurses, or a specific labor union. If you belong to one of these groups, a bank or credit union that offers these special programs might be the right mortgage provider for you. Some banks even offer special mortgage rates to people who already hold basic checking or savings accounts with the bank.

### Convenience is a key priority for you

There is definitely an air of ease that exists when your mortgage professional just happens to be sitting in the sales office at your new home community, or already has a working relationship with your builder, or is an employee of your personal bank. However, don't let ease alone sway you toward working with a bank representative. If you feel that you are being pushed into a type of loan that doesn't work for you because that happens to be the bank's specialty, or the bank is awarding a trip to Hawaii to the rep who closes the most of X type of loan—you should run screaming from the building! Working with most mortgage brokers is also very easy, logistically speaking, because most of the work can be done via phone, fax, mail, and e-mail. My favorite mortgage broker reports that she only meets 15% of her clients in person!

## Mortgage Brokers

Mortgage brokers work with independent mortgage brokerage firms that have relationships with many banks. Working with a mortgage broker is like having a personal shopper—they can get a good deal at Neiman's, Nordstrom, Target, Wal-Mart, and all your local boutiques. They can broker loans with the large, conservative banks, which tend to offer great interest rates and terms to the most qualified buyers. They can also broker loans with the smaller, local banks or more aggressive national lenders, which seek to provide mortgages to people who have less-than-perfect credit or less money for a down payment.

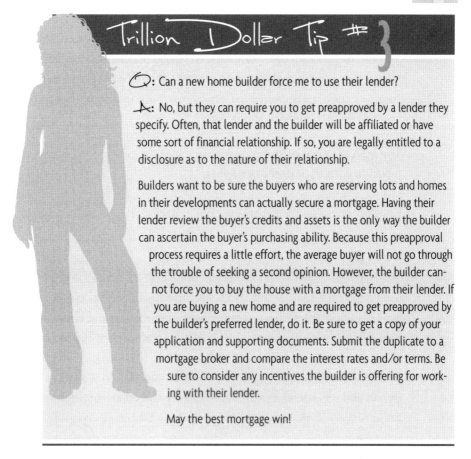

Trillion Dollar Tip #3

**Q:** Can a new home builder force me to use their lender?

**A:** No, but they can require you to get preapproved by a lender they specify. Often, that lender and the builder will be affiliated or have some sort of financial relationship. If so, you are legally entitled to a disclosure as to the nature of their relationship.

Builders want to be sure the buyers who are reserving lots and homes in their developments can actually secure a mortgage. Having their lender review the buyer's credits and assets is the only way the builder can ascertain the buyer's purchasing ability. Because this preapproval process requires a little effort, the average buyer will not go through the trouble of seeking a second opinion. However, the builder cannot force you to buy the house with a mortgage from their lender. If you are buying a new home and are required to get preapproved by the builder's preferred lender, do it. Be sure to get a copy of your application and supporting documents. Submit the duplicate to a mortgage broker and compare the interest rates and/or terms. Be sure to consider any incentives the builder is offering for working with their lender.

May the best mortgage win!

Rarely will you find a mortgage broker sitting at the lending desk in your new home community's model home. To find a reputable mortgage broker, just ask your real estate agent. Agents work closely and frequently with mortgage brokers, and they can hold them accountable for honesty and diligence in getting the mortgage funded in a way that a one-time or occasional client just can't do. You might want to work with a mortgage broker in the following instances.

### You have a special situation

If you are self-employed, or have some credit problems, or have a less-than-standard down payment, or are in need of an unusual or niche loan, a mortgage broker will be able to find multiple loans with lower interest rates and better terms. An example of a niche loan would be a 30-year, fixed-rate loan with an option to pay interest only for 10 years. Very few banks offer these types of loans, and it would be prudent to compare their rates and terms before selecting one. A mortgage broker will do the comparison for you.

### The builder is not offering incentives for working with their preferred lender

If there is no incentive to stay in house, you might as well seek a quote from an independent, outside broker with access to a wide universe of lenders and loan programs.

### You want someone who works exclusively for you, not the bank

Mortgage brokers are paid 100% on commission, and good mortgage brokers build their businesses through client referrals. If you're not happy with their offerings or can find a better loan elsewhere, they don't get paid—and they are well aware of this. As such, reputable mortgage brokers will aggressively look for the best loan you can qualify for, and will spend more time educating and counseling you regarding mortgage types and programs, because they hope you will work with them on and refer your friends and family members to them afterward.

### You are a stickler for getting the absolute best deal

Mortgage representatives and mortgage brokers will often offer very similar mortgage quotes to well-qualified buyers. However, with a mortgage broker there is more room for negotiating *origination fees* (the fee you pay them to do the loan) and getting competitive bids on interest rates. You should be realistic, though—no one is going to do your mortgage for free, and when seeking competitive mortgage quotes, you must compare apples and apples.

Whereas mortgage representatives are paid a combination of salary and commission, mortgage brokers are paid 100% on commission. When it comes to these commissions, for both types of mortgage professionals, the commission is usually a combination of monies paid by you and by the bank.

The fee you pay to your mortgage broker professional is called an origination fee, and is usually 1–1.5% of the mortgage loan amount. In the industry, each percentage point of the loan amount is simply called a *point*. The origination fee can range upward to as much as 2 or 3 points for hard-to-approve borrowers. However, if your mortgage professional proposes to charge you an origination fee greater than 2%, you should consider getting another quote or asking them if they can reduce the origination fee.

I recommend that you work with both types of mortgage professionals to start and narrow them down after you have a sense of who can provide the best deal.

## Builders 101

Builders fall into three major categories: custom, small volume, and production. Custom home builders build one-of-a-kind homes on land that is owned by the home buyer. Small-volume builders usually develop small subdivisions of fewer than 25 homes on land they own. Production home building companies are much larger and build anywhere from 25 to 25,000+ homes per year on land the company purchases. Production homes are built in accordance with plans created by the builder, although buyers may be given some options to alter floor plans and are usually allowed to select their own finish materials (e.g., tile, cabinetry, flooring, paint, etc.).

Many production builders employ sales representatives and design consultants within their new home communities. The primary goal of the sales representatives is to sell homes and get the transactions to close. The primary goal of the design consultants is to up sell you on everything from the actual house to the window treatments.

Therefore, it behooves you to walk into the model home with your real estate agent and a sense of clarity about what you are really looking for in your next home. If you walk in knowing you want the works, and you can afford it, great! But if you walk in knowing that your budget only allows for the standard items, you can save yourself (and the sales representative and design consultant) a lot of grief by being clear on your budget up front.

## Sales Representative

The sales representative is the person who greets you at the sales office when you first walk into a model home community. The sales representative will

- register you and your real estate agent on your first visit;
- tour the model homes with you, and explain the features and amenities, demonstrate how things work, and help you distinguish standard and upgrade items;
- answer any questions you have about the builder and the in-house or preferred lenders;
- tour the community with you, point out advantages and drawbacks of various lots and locations within the community, and answer any questions you have regarding soils, drainage, neighborhood rules and regulations; and,
- work with your real estate agent to draft the purchase contract and other agreements and explain these documents to you.

## Design Consultant

Some new home builders employ design consultants to help you with design choices. The design consultant will

- educate you on all of your appliance and finish material options and upgrades (e.g., tile, countertop materials, flooring, fixtures, etc.) and any floor plan customization options that are available to you;
- explain the pricing of the options and upgrades you select; and,
- document your selections and prepare any additional contracts or paperwork necessary to cement your selections and agreement to pay for them.

Make no mistake—the sales representatives and/or design consultants work for the builder. They are generally paid a base salary plus commission on the sale of upgrades, though some are paid on a commission-only basis.

## Construction Team

Although you won't be around to witness the vast majority of the things they do, these are perhaps the most important villagers. The construction team actually builds the frame, hammers in the nails, screws in the screws, connects the pipes, and runs the electrical wire (among other things) that, collectively, make up your new house!

The construction team comprises the builder/general contractor, superintendent, and trade contractor crews. You will become acquainted with the building or construction superintendent who will conduct walkthroughs with you, allowing you to view the structure of your home as it progresses toward completion. The superintendent's responsibilities extend beyond face time with customers. More than 200 individuals can be involved in the construction of a home, and at least 80% of them actually work on the job site. The superintendent directs and schedules the work they perform. The superintendent is a salaried employee of the building company and may also receive performance-based compensation or bonuses for completing the job on time, on budget, and with minimal punch list items.

# The Path Through the Village: The Process

The path through the village of professionals you have just met involves three phases:

1. preconstruction
2. construction
3. postconstruction

The process unfolds a little differently each time. However, there are 12 basic steps to the entire process—no matter what kind of new home you are buying or where you live.

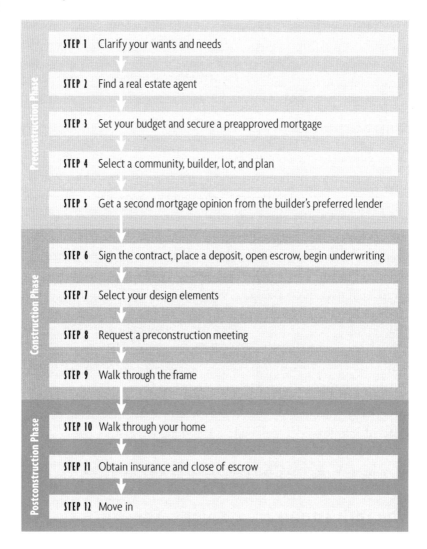

| | | |
|---|---|---|
| **Preconstruction Phase** | STEP 1 | Clarify your wants and needs |
| | STEP 2 | Find a real estate agent |
| | STEP 3 | Set your budget and secure a preapproved mortgage |
| | STEP 4 | Select a community, builder, lot, and plan |
| | STEP 5 | Get a second mortgage opinion from the builder's preferred lender |
| **Construction Phase** | STEP 6 | Sign the contract, place a deposit, open escrow, begin underwriting |
| | STEP 7 | Select your design elements |
| | STEP 8 | Request a preconstruction meeting |
| | STEP 9 | Walk through the frame |
| **Postconstruction Phase** | STEP 10 | Walk through your home |
| | STEP 11 | Obtain insurance and close of escrow |
| | STEP 12 | Move in |

## Preconstruction

### Step 1: Clarify your wants and needs

You began this process in Chapter 2 when you wrote down how you would like your life to be different after you are in your new home. Now it's time to get more concrete about translating your Vision of Home statement into a description of the house you want, complete with specific numbers of bedrooms and bathrooms, features, and amenities. It's also important to know what features and amenities are available to you, and to start getting a good idea of the square footage range you want. The easiest way to do this is to actually start visiting model homes and mentally linking the listed square footage with the reality of the corresponding physical space.

To help you firm up the details you seek, without getting overly restrictive, this book includes a *Home Buying Wants & Needs Checklist* in Appendix A. This checklist will help you communicate your vision to your real estate agent and other professionals who can help you find a community and a lot that matches your wishes.

### Step 2: Find a real estate agent

Some experts recommend that you interview 972 real estate agents and ask them each a long list of preselected questions. I disagree. Finding a good real estate agent doesn't have to be difficult or complicated. In fact, there are two tried-and-true methods of finding and selecting a real estate agent: referrals and seminars. Ask people you know and trust (friends, family, colleagues, clients, and associates from your church or temple) who their real estate agent was and what their experience working with them was like. Ideally, you should seek referrals from people who purchased new homes, but it's fine to seek referrals from those who bought resale too. You can also attend new home buying seminars and schedule an appointment with the presenters.

When meeting with prospective real estate agents describe your Vision of Home, and see if the prospective agent can catch on. You might also ask his/her opinion on how to decide between new and existing homes. A good real estate agent will be able to provide information on new home developments or established neighborhoods in the area that may offer the lifestyle you envision. Be conscious of your level of comfort as well; because you will be sharing your personal and financial information, you (and your spouse or other co-owner) should feel an interpersonal connection with the agent. Before you end the meeting, ask the agent to recommend an action plan for you. If you think the agent is competent and you are comfortable sharing your personal information with him/her and the agent came strongly recommended, then by all means you should work with the first person you interview. If not, continue to interview real estate agents until you intuitively know you've met a representative you feel good about.

### Step 3: Set your budget and secure a preapproved mortgage

Ask your real estate agent to recommend a mortgage professional and get preapproved at the maximum purchase price you can afford. The *Savvy Woman's Homebuying Handbook* provides a detailed, step-by-step tutorial on how to maximize your credit scores and other data and work with a mortgage broker.

## Trillion Dollar Tip #4

### Key questions to ask before you commit

**1.** What percentage of the homes have already been sold, and how many homes are left? Your home will not increase in value until the builder has sold all of the homes in the community. You don't want to end up with your home on the market in competition with the builder, who can sell brand new homes at the same price—or even less!

**2.** Will my home be part of a home owners' association (HOA)? If so, may I please read the HOA documents? HOAs can be great, and they can minimize the maintenance burden on you. But they often charge dues and impose restrictions on noise, parking, and the type of remodeling that you can do to your home. You need to know the details of any HOA regulations before you agree to be bound by them.

**3.** What other building and development is planned to take place in the neighborhood, district, or city? You don't want to buy a home because it abuts a lovely, green open space that is slated to house the region's largest 24-hour shopping, dining, and entertainment complex the very next year. Your builder's sales representative should be aware of upcoming developments in the area, years before ground is ever broken.

## Step 4: Select a community, builder, lot, and plan

With your real estate agent by your side, tour the new home communities in the area, which offer homes that meet your general wants and needs. Select the community, builder (some new home communities feature homes by several builders), lot, floor plan, and *elevation* (the look of house's façade from the street) that best fits your lifestyle needs.

## Step 5: Get a second mortgage opinion from the builder's preferred lender

Get a competitive mortgage quote from the builder's in-house or preferred lender, and compare it with the quote you got from the mortgage professional in Step 3. If you are struggling to decide between communities, builders, or lots, you and your real estate agent should compare builder incentives, and let the sales representatives know this will impact

## Trillion Dollar Tip #5

### Mortgage quotes: comparing apples with apples

When you get preapproved by a mortgage broker, make sure you request a good faith estimate. This type of quote is mandated by the U.S. Department of Housing and Urban Development (HUD). Its purpose is to provide more information about the loan than the average borrower would even know to ask for. It includes not only interest rates and repayment terms, but also a number of items related to the upfront costs of the loan.

When you get preapproved by a builder's preferred lender, ask them to also provide you with a good faith estimate. Then, and only then, can you meaningfully compare the two mortgage programs to determine which one is a better deal. Ask the mortgage professionals to explain the good faith estimate line-by-line. If it is unclear which mortgage is truly the best, ask your real estate agent to help you compare the good faith estimates.

your decision making. In today's buyer's market, one builder might offer some tempting incentive that will make your decision for you!

## Construction

### Step 6: Sign the contract, place a deposit, open escrow, and begin underwriting

Once you've selected a home, you will sign a construction and purchase contract that details both parties' obligations (yours and the builder's), documents the lot and home plan you've selected, and lists the date the builder predicts construction will be complete. Most builders will require you to remit an *earnest money deposit* (X percent of the purchase price) to indicate that you are serious about completing this transaction. Your deposit will be held in an escrow account with a neutral, third-party intermediary escrow or title company until later in the transaction, when it will be credited to your account, thereby reducing the cash you need for closing costs or a down payment.

You should select a mortgage professional and loan program just before or right after you sign your contract. Shortly after you sign your contract, your mortgage professional will request additional documents from you, such as paycheck stubs and bank statements, as the lender requests further information.

### Step 7: Select your design elements

This will vary by builder, but this is the point in the process when you select the colors and finish materials for the following categories:

- flooring
- cabinetry
- countertops
- fixtures and hardware
- lighting
- paint colors
- appliances
- window treatments

Most production home builders will allow you to make selections or upgrades in these basic areas. Some will even let you choose exterior materials, fireplace materials, sink types, and even stair parts! Some semi-custom home builders will give you floor plan and layout options.

Your contract will specify the date by which your design decisions must be made. Pay close attention to the *change orders* clause, which states that you agree to pay for any changes you make after you have submitted your design preferences.

To avoid costly change orders, make sure you are prepared for your design appointment. Do your research by visiting model homes. Decide what options and upgrades you want and write your wish list. Browse through interior design and home decor magazines and catalogs, and clip out pictures that evoke the feeling you want to create with your finish materials in your new home. Use your magazine clippings and wish list to prepare a dream home book, and take it to your design consultations.

### Step 8: Request a preconstruction meeting

Some builders offer this meeting as a matter of course; others don't unless you specifically request it. During this meeting, you will meet with the construction superintendent at your lot. This gives you an opportunity to see precisely how your home will be situated on the lot. The construction superintendent will brief you on the proposed construction timeline, educate you about the phases of the construction process and what you can expect in the upcoming weeks, and answer any questions you may have.

### Step 9: Walk through the frame

Different builders conduct walk-throughs at different points in the process. One of the most common site walk-throughs is the frame walk or frame walk-through. This walk-through will occur when the frame of your home has been erected and outfitted with electrical and plumbing, but before the walls are closed up. The construction superintendent will give you a tour and point out where each room and electrical feature will be located. I like to joke that a frame walk should start out like a wedding ceremony ends—with someone yelling, "speak now, or forever hold your peace!" Why? The frame walk is your last shot to check that the structural and electrical features of your home have been installed correctly and to your satisfaction; if not, now is the time to initiate corrections or changes.

At various other points during construction, you should feel free to schedule walk-throughs to check progress and see how you like recently installed components and finishes. But don't go overboard. Remember, time spent walking you through the house is time the superintendent can't be supervising the crew!

## Postconstruction

### Step 10: Walk through your home

When your home is finished, the construction superintendent and/or sales representative will take you on a final walk-through. Some builders call this walk-through a *home orientation*. You will tour all of the features of your home and receive instructions on how to operate emergency shutoffs. You will also learn how to use every appliance and system in the house. Finally, you will be asked to sign a completion report, which indicates that you are satisfied with your new home. A building inspector will inspect the property and give the final thumbs-up that the property is safe and suitable for occupancy.

### Step 11: Obtain insurance and close of escrow

You will obtain a policy of home owner's insurance, sign the final title and mortgage paperwork at the escrow company or attorney's office or in your home, and bring in your down payment funds either when you sign or submit it via wire transfer. The escrow holder will record the deed to the home with the county recorder's office on the next business day after your mortgage funds, making you the owner of record!

### Step 12: Move in!

The builder will give you the keys to your new home! On average, the home building process takes about 6–9 months. The process could be longer for a semi-custom home or a home built by a smaller builder or shorter for a home with few upgrades and options or for condos and townhomes.

Some trillion dollar women are intimidated by the prospect of navigating their home buying/building village. It may seem like all of the villagers outsmart you when it comes to their particular expertise. However, you are the only person in your transaction who is an expert on the only subject that matters: your family's wants and needs. With a PhD in lifestyle clarification, a master's in mindset management, a bachelor's in conscious competence, and a basic map of the path through the village, you are now utterly qualified to be the village chief!

# Remodeling Your Way

## The People and the Process of Drama-Free Home Improvement

The first big decision most would-be remodelers need to make is the decision whether they should remodel their existing home or move. If the remodel you envision is simply cosmetic, this decision may be a no-brainer. But if you're considering a major addition or dramatically reconfiguring your home, it might be a tougher call.

Some trillion dollar women approach this decision as a simple cost comparison: Would it cost me more to remodel or to move into a home that already meets my needs? For others, the monetary issues are more complicated, and there are many intangible and nonmonetary items to consider. Here are a few things to consider in the course of deciding whether to remodel or to move.

Most often, the remodeling project involves inexperienced, but passionate, home owners who are trying to get high-end work done for a discount price. However, your remodeling experience does not have to be one that involves you yelling random instructions to the construction crew in the kitchen, while you run your home-based business, prep the kids for tomorrow's tests, and squeeze in a cardio workout in the family room—all at the same time.

As a Realtor®, I have repeatedly seen homes put on the market mid-remodel, because the owners simply were exhausted and couldn't take any more, or ran out of money, or both. As a home owner and trillion

## The pros and cons of remodeling versus moving

| Factors in Favor of Remodeling | Factors in Favor of Moving |
|---|---|
| Your family doesn't need much more space, but the space you have needs to be updated. | Your family size has grown or decreased. |
| You love the precise location of your home and/or your school district, and very few homes in your neighborhood go up for sale. | You don't love your school district or neighborhood, and several homes are on the market. |
| Your kitchen and bathroom are outdated. | Your home is already the largest or most highly upgraded home for miles around. |
| You like your home's basic layout. | There are a number of homes on the market in your price range that meet your "dream home" characteristics, and your current home would take a lot of work to bring it to dream home status. |
| You are committed to living in your home for the rest of your natural life, because it has been in your family for several generations, and you love the 100-year-old oaks in the backyard. | You will have to move in the next few years. |
| You love the idea of remodeling your home. | You hate the idea of remodeling your home. |

dollar woman, I substantially remodeled my first home while I lived in it, and have remodeled other homes since. From all these experiences, I have derived one essential truth about remodeling—it does not have to be a chaotic process.

To have a successful, drama-free remodel, you must orchestrate the affair with intention and strategy, applying structure and organization to the process while retaining your ability to roll with the punches.

Envision the remodeling process as a stage production, in which you are the director. As such, you must know who the main characters are and what roles they'll perform. You might not need the entire cast, but you do need to know what they each do before you can make an educated decision one way or the other.

You will have a series of critical decisions to make in the course of directing this production. On most of them, there is no right or wrong decision, but there are a few things you should consider before making your decision and some predictable implications of each decision you make. In this chapter, you'll find some tools to help you make the best decision for you and your family.

## Meet the Cast

Unless you plan to do-it-yourself, your remodeling cast will be made up of at least some of the following characters. The nature and extent of your remodel will largely determine the types of professionals you'll encounter. For example, if you are simply having your bathroom painted and changing the fixtures, you'll only need painting and plumbing trade contractors. However, if you are building an addition to your home, you might need to work with the full cast.

### Mortgage Professionals

Many trillion dollar women fund their remodeling projects by taking a second (or third) mortgage or obtaining a line of credit against their home equity. We'll discuss these financing options in more detail in Chapter 5. Your mortgage professional—either a mortgage broker or a mortgage representative at the bank where you maintain your current home mortgage, checking, or savings accounts—will be involved in your remodeling project. If you don't currently have a relationship with a mortgage professional, seek referrals from your real estate agent or from friends and family members. You might also want to get a second mortgage quote from your regular lending or banking institution. See Chapter 3 for more information on mortgage professionals and for tips on how to compare mortgage quotes.

### Architects and Home Designers

These professionals share a few common functions. Architects and home designers help you

- conceptualize out exactly what you want out of your remodel;
- determine what needs to be done to your home to achieve the look, feel, and functionality you seek; and,
- create a set of written plans that communicate your vision to your contractors (and city permit personnel, if applicable).

In addition, these professionals will counsel you on and resolve any red flags or reasons your wishes might be infeasible. They will also eventually draw the final plans for submission to your contractors, and work with other industry professionals to ensure that your project complies with necessary building codes.

But there are also some key differences between architects and home designers. Architects are the most highly educated design professionals, holding at least a college degree and a state license. They specialize in helping you detail precisely what you want out of a structural change or addition to your home. Architects draw up the plans for your project and ensure that the plans are in compliance with building codes. An architect will list all of the materials that will be used and they detail the building specifications.

Many architects will also manage the project, including applying for permits, referring you to contractors and engineers, and even supervising the contractors throughout construction. On average, architects charge between 8 and 15% of the total cost of the project.

Home designers (or residential designers) are not generally licensed or regulated. Some have earned design degrees. They might also be certified by one of several professional organizations, including the American Institute of Building Design, the National Association of the Remodeling Industry, or the National Council of Building Design Certification. Home designers specialize in evaluating home owners' lifestyles and providing solutions for remedying dysfunctional floor plans. Some specialize in kitchen and bathroom design and many are knowledgeable in the latest home furnishings and appliances. A home designer will usually charge between 4 and 8% of the total cost of the project.

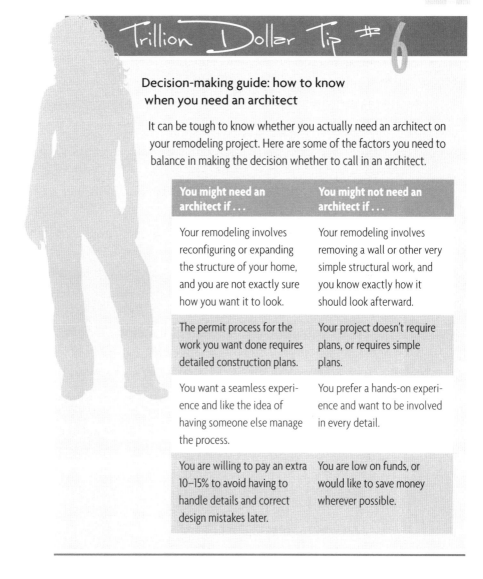

**Trillion Dollar Tip #6**

## Decision-making guide: how to know when you need an architect

It can be tough to know whether you actually need an architect on your remodeling project. Here are some of the factors you need to balance in making the decision whether to call in an architect.

| You might need an architect if . . . | You might not need an architect if . . . |
|---|---|
| Your remodeling involves reconfiguring or expanding the structure of your home, and you are not exactly sure how you want it to look. | Your remodeling involves removing a wall or other very simple structural work, and you know exactly how it should look afterward. |
| The permit process for the work you want done requires detailed construction plans. | Your project doesn't require plans, or requires simple plans. |
| You want a seamless experience and like the idea of having someone else manage the process. | You prefer a hands-on experience and want to be involved in every detail. |
| You are willing to pay an extra 10–15% to avoid having to handle details and correct design mistakes later. | You are low on funds, or would like to save money wherever possible. |

## General Contractors

General contractors coordinate and supervise construction labor during your remodel. Generally, they outsource individual tasks to trade contractors who specialize in a particular area, such as plumbing or electrical. Most states require general contractors to be licensed and to have insurance. General contractors are responsible for the following:

- creating and executing the sequence or timetable for the project
- hiring and supervising subcontractors
- supplying and supervising labor
- supplying equipment
- communicating with the design team to ensure that the work is completed according to your plans
- ordering and procuring construction materials

Recently, the construction industry has seen the emergence of a new one-stop provider: the design-build firm. This single company provides design and contracting services and will guide your project from start to finish. Beyond reduced total professional fees, the major advantage of working with a design-build firm is that you will be working with a cohesive team, which can result in less confusion, or contention, between an architect and a contractor who don't see eye to eye, thereby ensuring that the construction will be consistent with your plans.

Some design-build firms employ architects and licensed general contractors, whereas other general contracting companies have the ability to design and draw plans for simple remodels. Whether you hire a separate designer and contractor or a single design-build firm, be sure that you retain professionals whose aesthetics, ideas, and skills are aligned with your ultimate vision.

## Trade Contractors

Trade contractors (or trades) handle individual, specialized aspects of your remodeling project, such as the following:

- plumbing
- electrical
- roofing
- masonry
- flooring
- cabinetry
- fireplaces and chimneys

- lighting
- and anything else you can think of

Trades are generally supervised and scheduled by the general contractor. If you are going to be your own general contractor, or you have a project that is fairly simple, you might end up hiring and communicating directly with trade contractors about the details of your project.

## Structural Engineers

A structural engineer, like an architect, is a highly educated and licensed professional. You will need a structural engineer if your remodel entails significant structural alterations or additions to your home. Your architect will work with the structural engineer to ensure that the building plans are structurally sound. The engineer must stamp the plans with his state license number, as required by the city building/planning department, before your permits can be issued for work to proceed.

## City Building and Planning Staff

Interestingly enough, these cast members, who don't work for you, are the ones with the most potential to make or break your project. Depending on where your home is located and the provisions of your local municipal ordinance, your remodeling project may require that you obtain permission to remodel from your local building and/or planning department. There are three different types of staffers you might encounter to obtain permits for your project.

### Counter staff

These are the frontline staffers. They answer phones and staff the counters in planning and building department offices. Their role is to let you know if your project requires a permit and to provide you with the applications and guidelines for obtaining permits. For very simple projects, such as replacing a water heater, the counter staff may be able to actually issue the permit. For more complex and visible projects, a counter staffer might conduct a first-level review of your paperwork and photographs and put you through to the next level of review.

### City engineers

These professionals work behind the scenes to ensure that the plans for structurally, architecturally, or visually significant remodels comply with the city's building code. Many times, they have the final word on issuing the permit and authorizing work to proceed.

### On-site city inspectors

These professionals will actually visit your home before, during, and after construction to verify that the work is being completed as detailed in the approved plans. Often, the project will not be deemed permitted, or completed with a *finaled* (approved) permit, until a city inspector signs off on the finished product.

## The Remodeling Process: From Opening Act to Final Curtain

A successful remodel requires a sound strategy. It can be heartbreaking to get your project underway and then have it stop cold while you deal with something that should have been addressed earlier in the process. The following three-phased approach can help you make sure that as you go through the remodeling process, you'll experience much less frustration and much more success:

1. pre-remodel
2. remodel
3. post-remodel

Depending on the scope of your project, the process may involve more or less steps. In general there are 15 steps to the entire process, the majority of which will occur in the pre-remodel phase:

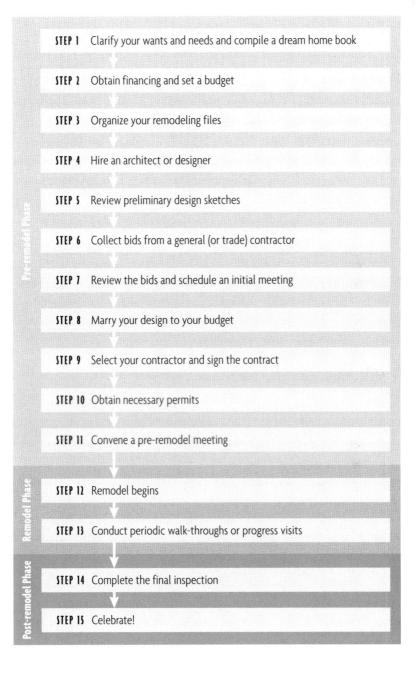

**STEP 1** Clarify your wants and needs and compile a dream home book

**STEP 2** Obtain financing and set a budget

**STEP 3** Organize your remodeling files

**STEP 4** Hire an architect or designer

**STEP 5** Review preliminary design sketches

**STEP 6** Collect bids from a general (or trade) contractor

**STEP 7** Review the bids and schedule an initial meeting

**STEP 8** Marry your design to your budget

**STEP 9** Select your contractor and sign the contract

**STEP 10** Obtain necessary permits

**STEP 11** Convene a pre-remodel meeting

**STEP 12** Remodel begins

**STEP 13** Conduct periodic walk-throughs or progress visits

**STEP 14** Complete the final inspection

**STEP 15** Celebrate!

Pre-remodel Phase

Remodel Phase

Post-remodel Phase

## Pre-remodel

### Step 1: Clarify your wants and needs and compile a dream home book

First, you have to be clear about how you want your home to be different after the remodel. You can get some great ideas by watching home design shows, visiting model homes and open houses, browsing home design and architectural publications and Web sites, and attending home shows. Collect photos and write descriptions of the features you want to duplicate or create in your own home to create a dream home book. Use this binder or scrapbook as a pictorial wish list. Your dream home book should also include a prioritized, comprehensive list of all the items you hope to change about your house or features you'd like to add or subtract during your remodel.

If you live in a community that is governed by a home owners' association (HOA), be sure to consult your covenants, codes and restrictions, which detail the alterations and remodeling you can make to your home, and add this information to your dream home book.

### Step 2: Obtain financing and set a budget

Clearly, if you are doing a small project, or you have come into an unexpected windfall, you might want to finance your project with your savings account. Many home owners use low or zero interest credit cards to finance midsize projects. However, if your project is a major remodel, you should consider borrowing against your home equity to finance the project. Your mortgage professional can educate you about the types of financing available and how a loan will impact your mortgage payments. Review your monthly budget to determine how much you can afford.

Once you are preapproved, your home's value will be appraised. Shortly thereafter, your mortgage professional will extend an offer that will consist of the total loan amount and the monthly payment schedule. You might choose to accept less than you are offered in order to keep your monthly payment low; but, you should come away from this step knowing how much money you can spend for your overall project.

Your budget should include a 15–30% cushion for changes and unexpected cost overruns. Before you make a final decision on your remodeling budget, you should consider the return on investment (ROI) you hope to recoup when you sell your home one day. A real estate agent's perspective can be invaluable in this step because over-improving a property (so that it is a hulking behemoth on a street full of cottages) can actually make it tougher to sell.

### Step 3: Organize your remodeling files

Centralizing all of the documents that pertain to your remodel is a sure-fire sanity saver. Purchase a 2-inch binder, a 3-hole punch, and dividers. Label the dividers as follows:

- brochures and bids
- correspondence
- contracts and addenda
- invoices and receipts
- miscellaneous
- permits and subdivision/HOA documents
- sketches and plans
- references
- schedules and timelines
- warranties

### Step 4: Hire an architect or designer

Seek referrals from friends, relatives, and colleagues. Most design professionals post their past projects and portfolios on their Web site. Search the Web for professionals who have similar aesthetic values to yours. Compile a list of three to five professionals, and call or e-mail them to request information about their services. Be sure to provide a brief description of the project you envision, your time frame, and the location of your home. At the very least, you should request a preliminary price/budget proposal and let prospects know when you plan to make a final decision.

During your initial meeting, give the prospective architect or designer a thorough tour of your home, with a special focus on the area(s) that will be remodeled, and show them your dream home book and wish list. Depending on the extent of your remodel, a good designer or architect may also want to do the following during the initial meeting:

- interview you and the other owner(s) to fully assess your goals for the project
- review any existing blueprints or plans for your home
- tour your lot
- measure rooms
- photograph the areas to be remodeled
- provide first-glance feedback on your project and its feasibility
- share their portfolio
- invite you to visit the site of current jobs
- provide references
- answer any questions you have

The American Institute of Architects offers a free online guide, *You and Your Architect*, at www.aia.org that provides questions you can use when interviewing designers and architects.

After you conduct your initial meetings, follow up! Check references and visit past job sites.

### Step 5: Review preliminary design sketches

Ideally, the presentation of your sketches will take place at your home, so that the designer or architect can help you get a sense for how the locations represented in the sketch correspond to the real life structure. Your designer or architect should provide one or more preliminary sketches or computer renderings of your project. You might receive several totally different concepts or several subtle variations on the same theme. The design professional should thoroughly explain the design to you. Request a few copies of the sketch so that you can take your time formulating thorough feedback to the proposed design.

> "Personal confidence in the architect is paramount. Seek also an appropriate balance between design ability, technical competence, professional service, and cost. Choose your architect at least as carefully as you would your doctor or dentist."
>
> *YOU AND YOUR ARCHITECT*

Unless you have a really strong, visceral positive or negative reaction to the design, hold off on providing feedback for at least a couple of days. Take a few days to discuss the preliminary design with your spouse, family, or other housemates. Mark up the sketches if you want to do something differently. Make a list on a separate sheet with your comments, questions, and concerns.

If you love the design, say so. If you hate it, say so. Do not be concerned that you might offend your design professional. Make sure you register every single concern, comment, or question—this empowers your design professional to make the revisions as close as possible to your vision as quickly as possible, and it will save time, money, and grief!

### Step 6: Collect bids from a general (or trade) contractor

Once you have preliminary sketch that represents your vision of home, you'll need an idea of the construction costs for your project. Collecting bids from prospective contractors can help you determine your costs. Use the same tactics you used in Step 4 to narrow down the field of prospects. Your architect or designer may be able provide a referral. You should get at least three bids from contractors who meet the following requirements:

- hold a valid state general contractor's license (ask for their license number, then verify that the license is current by visiting your state contractor's licensing board Web site)
- have worker's compensation insurance (ask to see an original certificate—not a copy)
- have a general commercial liability insurance with at least $1 million per incident coverage (again, ask to see the original certificate)
- have been in business at least five years (you do not want your project to be a learning experience)

Give each contractor a week to review your plans or propose their own plans/task list and submit an estimate, or you can have your architect or designer create a bid sheet that itemizes every task and material needed to complete the job (similar to the punch list), and ask the contractor candidates to fill in their bid for each line item. This way, you will get uniform bids that you can easily compare. However, you will lose some of the information you might otherwise have gleaned from the bid the contractor would have created from scratch. Some specialized and large firms prefer to use their own bid forms, so as to include their form legalese and verbiage. You can still give them your bid sheet and ask them to bid on the line items as well. Request that each contractor include a sample contract, proposed payment schedule, and a copy of their warranty.

### Step 7: Review the bids and schedule an initial meeting

Review the bids and read the contract and warranty. Be sure to get all of your questions answered before you make a final decision. There is rarely a super easy or obvious choice, but there are definitely other

Trillion Dollar Tip #7

**Should I disclose my budget to prospective contractors?**

Some contractors will ask you for your budget prior to submitting a bid. If you share it, three things could occur:

1. The contractor might bid higher because your budget is far greater than the work should cost.

2. The contractor might bid less because they are aggressively seeking new clients and hope to be the chosen bid.

3. The contractor might bid what they would have charged you without the information, but offer constructive suggestions for getting the bid down to your budget or point out how far under budget their prices are.

It would be wise to provide a ballpark figure in order to give the contractor a general estimate of your budget.

things that you should factor into your decision. See Appendix A for the *Contractor Evaluation Checklist*, which you can use when considering the intangible differences—above and beyond cost—between the prospective contractors.

If all of the bids are significantly over your budget, you may need to adjust your plans. This is also a good time to ask your prospective contractors to propose solutions for any foreseeable issues, including weather delays, labor issues, and supply shortages.

Schedule an initial meeting with the contractor who provides the best bid. Take your preliminary sketches or plans and dream home book to the meeting. The contractor should be able to tell you how long the project will take, when the work will begin, and how limited your access to areas of your home will be during the project. You should also find out if any elements of the project could be prohibited by your city or subdivision. If you need basic plans drawn, but you don't have a design professional, ask the contractor to draw the plans and provide an itemized task list (or punch list).

Request client references for recent and past jobs. Follow up with clients and, if at all possible, visit their homes. Be sure to ask if the job was completed on time and on budget and how the work has functioned over time. Finally, visit the Better Business Bureau's (BBB) Web site (www.bbb.org) to see if any complaints have been filed against the contractor.

### Step 8: Marry your design to your budget

Whether you are working with a design professional or working directly with a contractor, your plans will likely undergo several rounds of revisions, based on your budget and/or your preferences. The goal is for you to be 100% comfortable that the finished product reflects your wishes and fits within your budget.

### Step 9: Select your contractor and sign the contract

When you have selected your contractor, it is time to sign the contract. Unless it is a very minor remodel, you should hire an attorney to review it (a few hundred bucks to get the legal protection you need is worth it). Look for the following key items in your contract:

## Trillion Dollar Tip #8

**Bargain hunters beware!**

You should definitely take price into account when selecting a contractor, but do not let that be the deciding factor. If you approach the bidding process as a search for the lowest bid, you will inevitably get what you pay for.

The saying goes, "There are two professionals you should not ask for a discount: attorneys and plastic surgeons." I would add general contractors to that group. A discount contractor may not provide the quality, timeliness, and responsiveness you need for a project of this magnitude.

However, you should feel free to negotiate or to select the lowest bid if you are impressed with the contractor's professionalism, referrals, and past work.

- *contact information:* contractor's name, company, address and license number
- *scope of work:* details exactly what work they will do (and not do) and who is responsible (you or the contractor) for furnishing materials (finish and construction materials).
- *projected completion date:* specifies date and penalties for late completion or bonuses for early completion.
- *liability and liens:* details who is responsible if someone gets hurt onsite, and releases you from liability in the event the contractor fails to pay his suppliers or trades. (These groups can file a lien on your property, which will force you to pay them before you can sell or refinance your home, if your contractor owes them money.)
- *insurance and bonding:* details the type and amount of insurance and/or bonding the contractor will provide.

- *unexpected cost overruns:* details how unexpected costs will be handled.
- *finish materials:* details whether the finish materials will be paid for with an allowance or if specific brands and model numbers are to be used for each finish item.
- *work schedule:* details the days and times the crew will be on the job.
- *payment schedule:* details how you will pay the contractor. You might choose to pay upon completion of key segments of the job, or you might opt to open an escrow account, so that the escrow company is responsible for doling out the funds over time. Specifies whether an initial payment is required and when the work will begin. (Ideally, work should start the day the initial payment is made. It's a good idea to have payments tied to verified completion of different phases.)
- *warranty:* details the terms that apply to the labor and materials provided by the contractor, trades, and suppliers.
- *permits:* details who is responsible for obtaining permits (you, the architect, or the contractor). The contractor should guarantee that the work will pass inspections.
- *clean-up and debris removal:* details who will pay for and manage debris removal. Be sure that it stipulates that the contractor agrees to leave your home in broom clean condition.
- *alternative dispute resolution:* details how disputes will be resolved. In the event of a future dispute, you and the contractor either go to court or to have disputes mediated, arbitrated, or resolved by the BBB.
- *final payment:* specifies how the final payment will be paid. You may withhold 10–15% as the final payment, which will be paid when you have conducted a final walk-through and verified that every task is complete.

### Step 10: Obtain necessary permits

The permits should be obtained before work starts to ensure that the plans are approved without need for further revision. This can take a few minutes, hours, days, or months, depending on how involved the project is, how much it will affect the neighbors and the exterior appearance of the home, and how well your plans comply with the building code.

### Step 11: Convene a pre-remodel meeting

This on-site meeting should be attended by all of the players, so that you can collectively review the plans, construction sequence and timetable, finish material selections, and conduct a final plan and communication check to guard against miscommunications or misunderstandings.

## Remodel

### Step 12: Remodel begins

You would think that you could kick back and relax at this point, but that's not the way to go. Instead, refer to the following list of do's and don'ts to make sure things run as smoothly as possible.

### Step 13: Conduct periodic walk-throughs or progress visits

Schedule a time with your contractor to do occasional walk-throughs of the work area. For a kitchen or bathroom remodel, the entire project might only take a couple of weeks or a couple of days, so it may not make sense to meet 10 times. However, a major addition or full-home remodel may require a weekly walk-through. If your payment schedule was tied to the completion of certain tasks, you can use your progress visits to verify the completion of those tasks. As curious as you might be, resist the urge to visit or walk-through the work area all the time. Be available when the contractor calls, as they may need to inform you of an unexpected finding or get an answer from you.

## Post-remodel

### Step 14: Complete the final inspection

The team member responsible for permits arranges for the final inspection. After the inspection, you and your team will conduct a final walk-through to check your punch list and plans to make sure every task is complete. Make the final payment to the contractor only after you have verified that every single item is complete and the work areas are clean.

### Step 15: Celebrate!

Throw a post-remodeling soiree when you move back into the newly remodeled areas of your home, and show off your improved home to all your friends!

## Do's & Don'ts for a Smooth Remodel

**DO:** Monitor the schedule and check in often with your contractors to make sure your job stays on track or to make sure that you are aware of delays. Find out if any of your utilities will be shut off and when. You might need to be flexible regarding the precise completion date. If you had to temporarily move out, don't pack your things until your contractor tells you that you are less than a week away from completion.

**DON'T:** Make payments without verifying the corresponding tasks are actually complete.

**DO:** Show hospitality and appreciation to workers in your home. Make sure they know which restroom to use and, if possible, keep a pot of coffee or a bowl of fruit readily available. Greet them during your walk-throughs, and take notice of individual contributions. When people know their work is appreciated, they will do it with pride.

**DON'T:** Expect work areas to be spotless. Construction is messy, so let go of your inner Martha, and consider covering doorways or furniture with heavy sheets of plastic to prevent dust and debris from infiltrating your entire home. Treat yourself and have the entire house professionally cleaned when the job is done.

**DO:** Expect some delays and some cost overruns. Some industry insiders joke that every job takes 30% longer and costs 30% more than it was supposed to. I wouldn't say that's exactly true, but to expect everything to run perfectly on time and perfectly to the penny is to set yourself up for failure.

**DON'T:** Be surprised if you leave your precious belongings around and they get damaged. Put things away, or move them to an area far from the construction.

**DO:** If you live with others, designate one person to communicate directly with the general contractor, not the trade or the laborers.

**DON'T:** Go in and out of the work area, or allow your kids to do so. Most work sites have nails on the ground and are unsafe for children and adults without protective equipment.

**DO:** Develop and communicate house rules and routines for your family and the construction crew for the duration of the project. Designate which areas are work-free zones, and provide guidelines for parking and music volume for contractors.

**DON'T:** Be surprised at how stressful living through construction can be! Just plan for everything you can, stay flexible, expect the unexpected, and take extra care in selecting your professionals. If possible, take a vacation during the project, and give yourself a little break. What better excuse could there possibly be to go to a spa resort for the weekend?

## Congratulations—You Survived It!

With remodeling, you can't simply close your eyes and ride the wave through to completion. Even the word *remodeling* defies a simple definition. To one trillion dollar woman, it means painting some walls and laying some laminate flooring; to another, it means gutting the kitchen, moving walls, and adding a second floor master bedroom suite.

When your remodel is done, you might reflect on it and think it was a little anticlimactic. Two or three weeks later, you'll be using your new stainless steel chef's range or sitting at your custom built-in desk and you'll remember how you stressed and worried about how you were going to pull it off. Those memories of plastic-covered furniture and weekends spent picking tile will seem like they happened a lifetime ago. But you will have joined the ranks of trillion dollar women all over America who have managed to customize their homes without losing their sanity—or their shirts—without a PhD in home design or architecture. It turns out that just a little bit of conscious competence goes a very long way.

# CHAPTER 5

# Home Economics

## Finding the Funds to Buy or Remodel Your Dream Home

N ow it's time to discuss the most important ingredient of any successful new home purchase or remodeling project—money. Buying a newly constructed home trillion dollar woman-style is not about knowing everything there is to know about financing and mortgages. You just need to know a little bit about the resources available to you, and a lot about your own financial situation, so that you can be at peace with the new mortgage payment that comes along with your new home.

To remodel your home in true trillion dollar woman-fashion is about operating throughout your project from the calm place of abundant resources, rather than dwelling on the chaos that results when you try to get an MTV *Cribs*-worthy home on a *Design-on-a-Dime* budget! And like the new home buying trillion dollar woman, the remodeler trillion dollar woman takes care not to overextend herself, so she doesn't end up with a chrome, 6-burner gas restaurant range that gets used only to heat up pork-n-beans.

This chapter will provide useful tactics and tools to help you leap these building-related money matters in a single bound (or a couple of bounds, but you'll learn to leap them, and that's what matters)!

> ## The trillion dollar woman's survival kit
>
> - confidence
> - boldness
> - clarity on what you want
> - knowledge of what to expect
> - knowledge of the professionals involved
> - tools for making wise decisions
> - **money**

## New Home Economics

There are different loan types and considerations for financing a new home or remodel as opposed to financing an existing home. There are also unique challenges to creating a remodeling budget, determining your return on investment dollars, and managing the costs of new home options and upgrades. Let's start with the basics—a *mortgage* is simply the loan that is used to purchase the home. The mortgage (or loan) is secured by the home it was used to purchase. In laywoman's terms—if you stop paying the mortgage, the bank can take your home.

This explains why mortgage loans are the lowest interest-rate loans that are widely available; they present a very low risk to the lending institutions because the bank can always foreclose on the mortgage and own a very valuable asset if the borrowers default.

Well, this is not exactly true with new homes. Before building on the lot, the buyer may need to purchase the lot, which usually requires a bank loan. Then the buyer may need another loan to fund the construction of the home. Because the home is not yet built, there is nothing of value to secure the loan and minimize the risk to the lender. Generally speaking, loans for lots and for construction may require a larger down payment and charge higher interest rates than existing home mortgages. After the construction phase is complete, the buyer must secure a home mortgage, which entails going through the qualification, approval, and closing processes a second time.

## Construction-to-Permanent Loans: New Home Financing Solution

If you decide to buy a production home, chances are you will finance it with a *construction-to-permanent loan* (or two-in-one loans) this type of loan is a high-interest construction loan that converts to a low-interest home mortgage when your home is completed. Several national lenders offer construction-to-permanent loans for custom homes. This type of loan can also be obtained from most builders' in-house lenders and independent mortgage brokers. Here's how it works:

**STEP 1**   You apply for financing from the bank prior to signing a contract with the builder.

**STEP 2**   If your credit, income, assets, and job history are satisfactory—and the bank is satisfied with the reputation and stability of your builder—the bank approves the loan, which includes the price of the lot and construction costs.

**STEP 3**   Your builder and the bank negotiate a funds disbursement schedule (the funds are released as the home progresses toward completion).

**STEP 4**   Your home is completed.

**STEP 5**   City inspectors give it the thumbs up.

**STEP 6**   Your construction loan is paid off by the mortgage loan, which is now able to be secured by your new home!

There are numerous advantages to construction-to-permanent loans. For starters, there is usually only one closing, which not only saves time, but also saves money on escrow and title fees. With most construction-to-permanent loans, you only need to apply and qualify for financing once; rather than having to apply and qualify multiple times for the lot, construction, and mortgage, which saves money on origination fees.

Most banks offer these loans under their regular mortgage guidelines, rather than their standalone lot or construction loan guidelines, which might require a 30% down payment, or more! Banks often offer the same incentives, such as no down payment and lower interest rates, for these loans as for mortgages.

With construction-to-permanent loans, you are only required to pay interest during construction, rather than having to pay toward both interest and principal. Also, you are only required to pay interest on the funds that have actually been issued to the contractor. So, if your builder has only used $100,000 of the $600,000 it will cost to complete your home, you only pay interest on the $100,000 until the next disbursement of funds is made.

These loans may also provide you with a hedge against rising interest rates, and allow you to either lock in the interest rate for your permanent mortgage at the time you apply for the original construction loan or to lock your interest rate in anytime over the first 90 days of the construction loan. Once you lock in, your interest rate will remain the same if your home is completed within a certain period of time. If not, you can extend it for as long as your construction takes, for a fee.

The only real disadvantage to a construction-to-permanent loan arises if interest rates decrease during the time of construction. Also, committing to your mortgage in a two-in-one format limits your ability to shop aggressively for your eventual home mortgage.

If you are considering a construction-to-permanent loan, you will need to thoroughly consider mortgage terms of the loan to make sure that the mortgage is aligned with your lifestyle and your future plans.

The specific features of these construction-to-permanent loans vary from lender to lender; therefore, make sure that your mortgage professional explains every element of your loan. You should read every document you receive and get answers to all of your questions before you sign on the dotted line!

Speaking of all the dotted lines you will sign in the course of buying your new home, here are a few insider insights to help you keep your finances on track during your new home buying odyssey.

## Five Budgeting Need-to-Knows for Buying a Newly Constructed Home

### #1: *Know your numbers*

Before you sign a contract or a loan application, you should know your critical personal financial numbers. At the very least, before you even start looking for a new home you should write down the answers to the following questions for every borrower that will be on the mortgage:

a. What are your FICO [credit] scores? Check it at www.annual-creditreport.com. This government-mandated site allows you to get a free copy of your credit report every year. Make sure you order the reports and scores from all three credit reporting bureaus (Experian, EquiFax, and TransUnion).

b. What is your annual pretax income?

c. What are your monthly debt payments? Include credit cards, lines of credit, auto loans, and student loans.

d. What assets do you own, and what is their value? Include your current home (if you own), checking and savings accounts, retirement accounts, and traded assets (e.g., stocks and bonds).

e. What is the maximum amount you are able to spend monthly on housing?

f. Does that amount include taxes, insurance, and HOA dues? Can you come up with extra cash for these items, or do you need to keep your mortgage payment low enough that these items can be included in your answer to question (e)?

If you bring this information to your mortgage professional, he or she will get you preapproved and give you a price limit for how much you can spend and still stay within your household spending plan.

### #2: Get preapproved before you get in the car

Don't even get in the car to go house hunting until you get approved for a loan. Why? Because there's only one thing worse than falling in love with a house and learning later that it's way out of your price range—and that's deciding to buy a house you really can't afford. After you see an $800,000 house that you can't afford, the $300,000 one you can afford may not look so good!

### #3: Understand the pricing

In this one way, shopping for a new home is like shopping for a new car. A few consumer-friendly builders have adopted a model-is-standard approach, but for the most part, the models you walk through may have thousands of dollars in optional features and upgrades. The base price often includes few, if any, of the features that may have made you fall in love with the house. Ask the sales representative to point out the upgrades and options. Then ask the price of your new home with all the upgrades that are on the model, so that you will know how much more over the base price you might pay for your finished home. You might consider looking at homes with starting prices that are 10, 20, or even 30% lower than your purchase price limit in order to be able to upgrade your home and stay within your budget.

### #4: Be budget conscious when shopping for options and upgrades

One of my personal financial advisors likes to say, "Don't check out at the checkout counter." It is very easy to get caught up in the ultimate shopping spree when you are selecting your finish materials. On a nice-sized, $400,000 home anywhere in America, you can easily walk in intending to spend $50,000 on upgrades and walk out an hour later having spent $150,000. When selecting upgrades, you should stay within the total home purchase price range that suits your budget, which means you might need to choose between a more modest house with luxurious finishes and a luxury home with more modest finishes. Visit the model home and list all of the finish materials you want ahead of your design appointment. Send your list and your model and/or floor plan to the design consultant or sales representative in advance of your appointment, and ask the consultant or sales representative to send you an upgrade cost estimate a few days before your appointment. If you can afford them all, great! If not, you'll have time to prioritize and decide what you must have and what you can sacrifice.

### #5: Save money by asking for incentives

When there are more new homes slated for construction than there are buyers, builders often offer incentives before they offer discounts. Common buyer incentives include:

- closing cost credits (the builder will pay 3% or more of the purchase price to cover your loan fees, escrow and title costs, and even some city or county transfer taxes)
- home owners' association (HOA) dues (some builders will pay as much as one or two years of your HOA dues)
- design credits (I've seen builders offer $10,000–$50,000 in credits for upgrades)

Each of these incentives saves you literally thousands of dollars. Be sure to ask your real estate agent and your builder's sales representative what incentives you can get before you sign the construction and purchase contract.

## Finding Funds for Remodeling

I meet would-be trillion dollar women all over the country. They say they would love to remodel their homes, but they don't have the money. The truth is, most inexperienced remodelers overestimate what their remodel will cost. Although Baby Phat design mogul Kimora Lee Simmons might spend $100,000 to remodel her kitchen, the average trillion dollar woman will spend roughly $20,000 for a minor kitchen remodel. You might not have $20,000 just lying around, but you do own a home. Owning a home and/or having great credit might mean you do have the cash you need at your fingertips.

According to the Harvard Joint Center for Housing Studies, the top three ways home owners fund their remodeling projects are (1) savings, (2) credit cards, and (3) borrowing against their home equity.

If you have the cash in savings to spare—you rock! Just make sure your savings account is not bone-dry at the end of your remodel. Keep a little cushion of cash tucked away for a rainy day (preferably in a high interest rate, liquid account). If you don't have the cash, all is not lost; you just need to consider financing some or all of the costs of your remodel.

Home owners who want to do a remodel that costs less than $10,000 typically use credit cards to finance the project. Credit cards can also be a great tool to finance your project, if used correctly. Using a credit card to finance your remodel simply requires that you have a clear understanding of the credit card terms and your monthly finances. Create—and stick to—a repayment plan, especially if you want to avoid paying interest; and don't just make the minimum payment on the card. If you do, you could end up paying 3 or 4 times the amount of your remodel by the time you are done paying interest.

If you are using a 0% interest card, pay close attention to when the interest kicks in. With store cards in particular, that 0% interest can convert in the blink of an eye to 18, 21 or even 24% interest! The benefits of using the credit cards offered by the stores are defeated if you allow the balance to begin accruing interest.

For example, you want to remodel your bathroom with a new bathtub (with jets), toilet, vanity, flooring, paint, and light fixtures. The local home improvement store gives you an estimate of $9,600 for the work (it's a small bathroom). The store offers you a credit card that charges 0% interest for the first 12 months. You do the math and figure out that you will have to pay $800 per month to avoid paying interest. You usually spend about $500/month on non-essential items such as books, cable, smoothies, and coffee, and $300/month eating out for lunch. By giving these things up for one year, you could soon be spending your evenings luxuriating in your Jacuzzi tub, reading books that you checked out from the library, and a year later you will have paid for your new bathroom.

## Home Is Where the Money Is:
## Using Home Equity to Fund Your Remodel

For major remodels, the most popular sources of funds are financing products that are secured with home equity. That is, loans that (like mortgages) are secured by your home. Banks readily lend large amounts of money on these types of secured products at very low interest rates because they tend to be low risk loans for the bank. The definition of home equity is simple: Equity is the difference between what your home is worth and what you owe on it.

For example, if your home is worth $265,000 and your current outstanding mortgage debts total $142,000, you have about $123,000 in home equity at your disposal. But it's not just free money. In order to get liquid cash out of your equity, you must either (a) sell your house or (b) get a loan that is secured by your equity. If you wanted to do (a), you wouldn't be reading this book, and if you do (b), there is always a monthly loan payment associated with that decision. You will have to decide whether you are willing to pay toward another loan and, if so, how much more you can afford to pay.

One advantage of borrowing against your home equity to fund your remodel is that the interest you are charged is probably tax deductible as mortgage interest. You should discuss your plans for financing your project with your tax advisor before you commit to anything.

There are four different vehicles that allow you to harness the power of your home equity and transform it into cash to remodel your home:

### #1: Home equity loan

This very simple loan is also called a *second mortgage*. The lender appraises your home, assesses what you currently owe on your home, and offers you a check in the amount of some or all of your home equity. You make monthly payments that include interest and some of the principal, until the loan is paid off. Most home equity loans charge a fixed interest rate so you can predict your payment and your interest for the life of the loan.

### #2: Home equity line of credit (HELOC)

A HELOC is just like a home equity loan with one nice exception—it offers a revolving line of credit. So, as you pay your balance down, more credit becomes available for you to use again. Unlike a home equity loan, you will not just receive a big check. Instead, you generally get a debit card and checks that you can use to get cash or write checks up to the limit set by the bank. Also, you only pay interest on your balances. A HELOC allows you to have instant access to funds without paying interest on funds that you are not currently using. You can save quite a bit of money with a HELOC if you get approved for your financing months before the construction begins and the spending commences. The one catch is that the interest rate on most HELOCs is adjustable, so it fluctuates monthly based on the market. However, there are caps on how much your rate can rise in a year and over the life of the loan.

### #3: Cash-out refinance

Many trillion dollar women with less-than-ideal credit or very little money for a down payment have used this option to finance their remodel. Depending on the rate and terms of your current mortgage versus the rate and terms for which you and your home now qualify, it may be prudent to refinance your entire mortgage and pull some cash out at the same time. If your new loan significantly lowers your interest rate or otherwise changes your payment terms, you might actually be able to keep your payment the same—or even lower it—while pulling out funds. However, make sure you understand the terms of your new mortgage, and that the new lower payment will not create an increasing loan balance or some other problem for you.

### #4: Construction loan

If your remodeling project is really expensive or you don't have enough home equity to cover it, you might be a good candidate for a construction loan or a construction-to-permanent mortgage. Because these are not true equity loans, the interest rates might be higher, but if the remodel will result in a major increase in the value of your home, it might be worth considering.

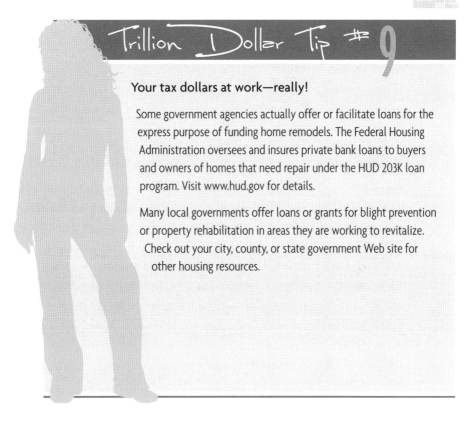

## Trillion Dollar Tip #9

**Your tax dollars at work—really!**

Some government agencies actually offer or facilitate loans for the express purpose of funding home remodels. The Federal Housing Administration oversees and insures private bank loans to buyers and owners of homes that need repair under the HUD 203K loan program. Visit www.hud.gov for details.

Many local governments offer loans or grants for blight prevention or property rehabilitation in areas they are working to revitalize. Check out your city, county, or state government Web site for other housing resources.

## Five Budgeting Need-to-Knows for Remodeling Your Home

### #1: Budget for surprises

I know I've said this several times, but it cannot be overemphasized. I have heard of maybe one remodel in my entire career that has actually run under budget. Some remodels do run on budget, and those contractors get huge kudos from me. But many, many remodeling projects run over budget, and if it happens to you it can be an unwelcome surprise. In fact, you should really plan to go over budget, and set aside a budget reserve of 10–30% for cost overruns. Selecting and pricing your finish materials before you sign an agreement with the contractor can also minimize the chances of surprises.

### #2: Capitalize on your contractor's shopping discount

Most home improvement stores offer a frequent shopper/professional discount to contractors. Find out if your contractor has any such arrangement and which store or stores honor it. Then, select your finish materials and use their discounted prices in the contract—you could save 15% or more.

### #3: Shop online

If you live in a high-cost area, you might be paying a premium for your materials because the store or warehouse has to pay high rents. Consider shopping for materials online. If you just have to see the items in person, write down the brand and model numbers of your favorite fixtures on display at the local hardware store, then search for them in your favorite search engine. You can save tons of money, and if you don't need to go see them in person first, you might save tons of time, too! (And you can get your shopping done in your pajamas, with no makeup on.)

### #4: Account for incidentals

Remodeling costs are not limited to what you pay for labor and materials. If you have to move out of your home during the remodel, make sure your relocation costs fit in your remodeling budget. If you live on a block with parking restrictions and time limits that you know the concrete trucks or debris containers will violate, create a small budget allowance for traffic tickets.

### #5: Avoid change orders

Sometimes changes are unavoidable, such as when the contractor finds rot and must repair an area before moving forward. However, changes are often the result of home owners making a change to the original plans. When this occurs, the contractor will issue a *change order*. The cost of the task in any given change order can be drastically higher than the cost of that task if you had included it in the original punch list or bid sheet. A few seemingly small changes can skyrocket your construction costs and shatter your budget. Take your time and make sure your plans reflect your vision of home before you put it out to bid.

### Is it worth it?

Every remodeling project begs the same question: Is it worth the money? Different people define worth differently; for example, if you plan to live in a home for 15 years and your family swims a lot, installing a pool might be "worth it" for you, even if you don't recoup your investment when you resell the home. Savvy remodelers often do want to know how much they can expect their remodel to increase the value of their home. Asked differently, how many of your remodeling dollars will be recouped when you sell your home?

*Remodeling Magazine's* annual Cost vs. Value report is the authoritative source for projecting the return you can expect on your investment in your home. It lists the percentage of your remodeling costs that you can expect to recoup by project type (e.g., siding replacement, new windows, kitchen remodel, etc.). No remodeling project will return more money than you spend on it. But when you factor in the intangible value of your family's ability to enjoy living in your remodeled home, a 70 or 80% return on your remodeling investment may make it more than worth your while! For specific numbers, check out: www.remodeling.hw.net.

Now that you understand what's available, take the quiz on the next page and find out which financing option will work best for your needs.

## QUIZ   How should I finance my remodel?

Circle the letter that best describes your financial situation.

A   You don't need the tax deduction.

B   You are eligible for a low or zero interest credit card that will cover the remodeling costs.

C   You know exactly how much you will need.

D   You may not need to spend as much as you are offered.

E   Your home doesn't have sufficient equity to fund the entire remodel.

F   Your property is in need of non-cosmetic repairs.

---

A   You have plenty of cash in reserve.

B   You have room in your monthly budget to pay the charges down or off before you are charged much interest.

C   You dislike the idea of paying an adjustable interest rate.

D   You can use the additional mortgage interest tax deduction.

E   Your remodel is a major project.

F   Your property is located in an area that is being revitalized.

---

A   You can fund the project without depleting your emergency reserves.

B   You are financially disciplined and will stick with your own repayment plan.

C   You don't mind paying interest on the whole amount all the time.

D   You are financially disciplined, and will not spend the funds on things like vacations and depreciating assets like cars.

E   Your remodel project will add significantly to the value of your home.

F   Your household income could be described as low to moderate.

A     Your remodel is a small project.

B     You don't have many other credit cards with balances at or near their credit limits.

C     You are financially disciplined, and will not let the money run through your fingers.

D     You owe quite a bit less on your home than it is worth on today's market (i.e., you have substantial home equity).

E     You can afford to pay the higher interest in addition to your current mortgage for the duration of the construction project.

F     You don't plan to use your home as a rental property anytime soon.

---

If you circled 3 or more of choice A—You probably have enough savings to finance your remodel.

If you circled 3 or more of choice B—You're probably disciplined enough to finance your remodel using a credit card.

If you circled 3 or more of choice C—A home equity loan will be your best bet.

If you circled 3 or more of choice D—You probably need the flexibility of a HELOC.

If you circled 3 or more of choice E—A construction loan will help you finance the remodel of your dreams.

If you circled 3 or more of choice F—You should research and take advantage of a government loan.

## The Toolkit and Caboodle

Far be it from me to say that the money area is the most fun or exhilarating piece of your home buying or remodeling adventure. However, it is probably the most necessary piece. Without the money, nothing happens. Now that you understand where to get the money you need, what things to think about and look for when you are offered the money, and how to best budget your funds we can move on to the stuff which probably inspired you to take on your new home or home renewal project—the features, amenities and design elements, which can make life so much easier and more beautiful.

# CHAPTER 6

# Trillion Dollar Woman Profiles

## Secrets for Aligning Your New Home Life with Your Personality, Values, and Lifestyle

A trillion dollar woman defines success at creating her new home environment in terms of lifestyle enhancement—how much easier, more beautiful, or more enjoyable life will be in her new or remodeled home than it was before. Therefore, in order to achieve success, you must know your profile.

Knowing your profile will help you select finish materials, options, and upgrades for your new home; develop your vision for your existing home's remodel; ensure that your new home environment makes your life better in ways that you value; prioritize your spending plan for your new home or remodeling project; and save you time, money, and energy as you communicate your vision to the design and construction professionals who will help you manifest it. To determine your profile, consider your motivations and priorities for your home. You will need to think about

- which rooms you remodel or upgrade, and why;
- what you want to do to those rooms or areas;
- where and how you will spend money in some areas, relative to others; and,
- which finishes and design elements you will incorporate into your home.

## A Tale of Two Closets

Our first home was a moderate fixer-upper. It was all we could afford and we did most of the work ourselves. When we bought our next home, we chose one that needed very little work. The previous owners had converted an adjoining small bedroom to create a wide, rectangular closet, with doors, in the master bedroom. However, they did not install a single rod to hang clothing. So, we decided to hire a contractor to install an organizational system.

I always dreamed of one of those fancy custom closet organizational systems. We had attempted to install one in our previous home, but it fell apart whenever we put more than three pairs of jeans in the closet!

I called a custom closet contractor, and they sent out a consultant who was absolutely amazing. She marched into the closet, took all sorts of measurements, and asked us about our storage needs and clothing. She then drew a detailed diagram of the closet.

After she sketched out few designs, we selected the finishes we wanted and reviewed the pricing, contract, and timeline; she reluctantly made one more request. She wanted to measure our shoes to ensure that she would get our storage needs just right. Impressed with her attention to detail, we let her measure our shoes. Shortly thereafter the closet system was installed and we have been thrilled with it ever since.

So when my mother started complaining about her closet chaos a few years later, I instantly referred her to the same company. She called them and was visited by a different, yet still amazing, consultant who asked her all sorts of seemingly bizarre questions. My mother's closet is very different from ours. It's tall, narrow, and round. Whereas, I keep all clothes for all seasons in my closet, my mom rotates her out-of-season items into another closet, and she keeps her Imelda-esque shoe collection neatly organized.

The closet specialist built her a custom closet that she absolutely loves. They took advantage of her closet's unique space and installed hydraulic-powered rods that she can raise and lower, and a shepherd's hook that allows her to reach the higher shelves in the closet.

I had a home design epiphany after our two distinctly dissimilar closet design experiences. Although my mother and I are two very different women, with very different lifestyles and needs, we were able to benefit from the same solution. Our closet organizers made both our lives much easier. The key to our successful experiences was customization, facilitated by the astute questioning of the closet consultants. They asked exactly the right questions to develop a profile of each of us, and from that profile they devised precise, effective solutions to our problems (some of which we didn't even know we had).

But don't put the book down and start measuring your closet just yet. I've developed three personality profiles based on the thousands of trillion dollar women who I've met during the course of my career: the serenity seeker, the clever utilitarian, and the sophisticated entertainer. Review all three to determine which one best describes you.

## Trillion Dollar Woman Profiles

#1 The Serenity Seeker

**Who is she?** She is your garden-variety, super busy woman.

**What does she want and need?**

- a sense of serenity, relaxation, and calm
- a place to recharge so she can meet the demands of her daily life
- a little indulgence (depending on her personality, she might want a few creature comforts or total, over-the-top luxury such as a full-blown indoor spa with sauna, Jacuzzi, massage table, and yoga room)
- a private place of her own where she can unplug and decompress

**Rooms and areas of primary concern:**

- master bedroom suite
- mind-body fitness room
- private rooms or areas, including her closet

**Design preferences:**

- design elements that control clutter and create clear boundaries between functional and restful areas

**Favorite home improvement show:** *Breathing Room*

**Celebrities she channels:** Madonna or Gwyneth Paltrow, retreating to the English countryside to take a break from the demands of stardom.

**Remodeling/home trends she loves:**

- rejuvenation room for yoga and meditation
- spa bathroom complete with spa shower or sauna
- snoring room (a private bedroom or sitting room in the master bedroom suite)

**Views her home as:** her sanctuary

# #2 The Clever Utilitarian

**Who is she?** She is either the busy mom whose primary concern is making sure everyone else has the space to do what they need to do, or the hip, urbanite who lives in such small quarters that function takes precedence over form.

**What does she want and need?**
- a simplified life
- a way to prevent chaos
- a place in the home for everything, everyone, and every activity

**Rooms and areas of primary concern:**
- common areas such as living and family rooms
- function-specific rooms such as the kitchen and office

**Design preferences:**
- design elements that foster organization and provide storage solutions

**Her favorite home improvement show:** *Extreme Home Makeover*

**Celebrity she channels:** Why, Martha, of course! (And MacGyver a little bit, too, but don't tell anyone.)

**Remodeling/home trends she loves:**
- built-in everything, from desks to garbage and recycling stations
- closet and garage organizers
- heated sidewalks in snowy climates to minimize shoveling

**Views her home as:** functional space for the tasks of daily living

# #3 The Sophisticated Entertainer

**Who is she?** She ranges in age from 20 to 80. She is self-assured and opinionated. Quality is important to her; she is the tastemaker in her crowd and she enjoys entertaining in her fabulous home. She is an early adopter of home technologies and all things swank.

**What does she want and need?**

- the best, latest, and most luxe styles and models of everything for her home
- open, comfortable spaces that are conducive to entertaining

**Rooms and areas of primary concern:**

- kitchen and dining room
- great room
- living room
- outdoor areas suitable for entertaining

**Her favorite home improvement show:** *Cribs*

**Remodeling/home trends she loves:**

- outdoor fireplaces and kitchens
- high-end gourmet kitchen/great room combos
- home theaters

**Celebrity she channels:** Oprah (especially when her party planner dissects holiday dinners on the show).

**Views her home as:** her showplace

## What's Your Profile?

Most trillion dollar women read these profiles and immediately identify more strongly with one than the others. Or you might find, like most, you share traits of all three, which would make you a serenity seeking, utilitarian, entertainer.

Now you can start to isolate your priorities in terms of the specific items, amenities, features, and finishes you'll want in your new (or newly remodeled) home, room-by-room and on the exterior of your home. Before you make your design selections or create your remodeling dream book, you'll want to consider your profile and a set of questions particular to each area of your home. This way, you'll make conscious choices that will keep your new home environment in alignment with your values, lifestyle, and personality.

## Room-by-Room Consideration Questionnaire

### MASTER BEDROOM

1. Is there sufficient closet and storage space? Is it well-organized and usable?

2. Does your master bedroom contain a bathroom? If so, what enhancements do you want to make to it? If not, do you want one?

3. Do you want a separate area for dressing or reading?

4. What home electronics and entertainment media will you have in your room?

5. Where will you place those items?

*If you identified as a serenity seeker:* Consider carving out a private retreat area, perhaps an adjoining room or a space within the master bedroom. If you have electronics in your room such as a television and DVD player, consider creating built-ins or using furniture that can completely conceal these items at bedtime. Built-in drawers and closet organizers can be used to conceal much of your personal clutter that might otherwise disrupt your relaxation and sleep.

*If you identified as a clever utilitarian:* Like the serenity seekers, you should consider closet organizational systems and built-in clothes storage systems, so that everything will have a proper place. Built-ins also minimize the furniture you have to buy, move, dust, and maintain.

*If you identified as a sophisticated entertainer:* You are most likely to have a gas burning fireplace in your master suite that is timed to ignite and heat your room before bedtime. Similarly to the serenity seekers and clever utilitarians, you might consider a custom closet organizational system complete with high-end finishes, and enough shelving to display your haute couture wardrobe.

## Children's Bedrooms

1. How many children do you have (or want)?

2. What are their ages?

3. What are their hobbies and interests?

4. If sharing a room, how many children will sleep in the room?

5. How much closet space does each child need?

6. Will the children study in their rooms?

7. Will there be a television in the room?

*If you identified as a serenity seeker:* You might want the children's rooms to be located at some distance from your room depending on the age of the children.

*If you identified as a clever utilitarian:* You will want to create boundaries that define the space that belongs to each child, in terms of sleeping, storage, study, and play areas.

*If you identified as a sophisticated entertainer:* You will want to create an entertaining environment for your children. You are likely to decorate and furnish your children's rooms in accordance with a theme such as pirates, princesses, or sports depending on the child's interests.

## Bathrooms

### Master Bathroom

1. Do you want to remodel the bathroom and replace the sink, shower, and toilet, or do you want to enlarge the bathroom and change the layout?

2. Where will you store your bathroom supplies?

3. Do you want to change your outside view or prevent passersby from looking inside?

4. Would you like dual sinks, vanities, and/or medicine cabinets?

5. How much mirror space and lighting do you need?

6. How open to or separate from the master bedroom should this room be?

7. Do you need a separate shower and bath?

8. Do you need a bathtub?

9. What else do you use your bathroom for (get dressed, apply makeup, lounge around)?

10. Do you need storage space for cosmetic appliances such as curling irons and blowdryer?

11. Do you have sufficient lighting for your mirror?

## Other Bathrooms

12. How many children will be using the bathroom?

13. How old are they and how much longer will they be living in the home?

14. Where will bath linens be stored?

*If you identified as a serenity seeker:* Consider outfitting your master bath with speakers, sauna or steam shower features, and clawfoot or therapeutic jetted bathtubs. You might like a private window that looks out onto an outdoor fountain or even a window with glass blocks to let light in but maintain privacy. You may also want room for a chaise lounge or vanity. In terms of other bathrooms, just make sure there is another bathroom because you definitely need your own.

*If you identified as a clever utilitarian:* If you take showers, consider a large tiled shower with glass doors and a tiled bench seat for shaving and storing bath products (and that squeegee you'll no doubt keep inside). Also, look for additional shelving and cabinetry and dual vanities (if you share the bathroom). In terms of other bathrooms, you'll want to ensure that each child has at least their own cabinet and drawer and perhaps even their own vanity (or bathroom, if possible). The other bathroom should also have a small storage space for supplies.

*If you identified as a sophisticated entertainer:* Your bathroom is likely to include a two- or three-person Jacuzzi tub with extra jets with a separate stall shower and a fireplace. Like the rest of your home, your guest bathroom is likely to include high-end finishes such as detailed tile work, granite counters, and top quality wood cabinets, as well as luxury touches such as glass bowl sinks with sensor-operated faucets.

### KITCHEN

1. Who is the primary cook?


2. Is he or she right- or left-handed?

3. Does anyone usually help with the cooking?

4. Does the cook also bake?

5. Is there sufficient space in the pantry for food storage?

6. Is the food preparation space sufficient?

7. Is the workspace triangle—the area from refrigerator to counter-top to stove—too big?

8. Do you have sufficient space to store appliances and gadgets?

9. Do you prefer to have those items out on the countertop or stored behind closed doors?

10. Do you prefer to have a separate dining area?

11. Or would you like to have an informal dining area in your kitchen as well as a formal dining room?

12. Do you shop for food in bulk?

13. Do you entertain often?

14. Do you employ caterers?

*If you identified as a serenity seeker:* Your kitchen needs are all about ease and calm. Consider creating extra cabinet space to store coffee and bread machines, as you might dislike seeking the clutter they can create on the countertop. Having several cabinet doors with glass fronts can create an open and airy feel.

*If you identified as a clever utilitarian:* You might like an enclosed kitchen that can be closed off to company if the kids make a mess. Extra cabinetry and pantry space will allow you to stock up on basic staples. To make the most of wall space, you might install under-the-sink sponge drawers that tilt out under the sink, Lazy Susan corner cabinets, built in spice drawers, and large pullout drawers for pots and pans. A built-in recycling and garbage system can help you ensure that the trash is in its right place. Such a system can also encourage your family to recycle.

***If you identified as a sophisticated entertainer:*** Your kitchen will probably be outfitted with a six-burner, restaurant-grade stove with matching range hood, and decorative, lit cabinetry. The room will probably include specialty cabinets or drawers, such as cookware drawers, slide-out spice racks, and/or an island with a butcher-block top. Whether you cook or not is irrelevant—the caterers might need a large capacity fridge to serve your guests. A kitchen that flows into an adjoining living or dining room or has a pass-through bar might be just the ticket for your parties and events.

## COMMON AREAS

1. Do you prefer to have one open, casual common area or separate formal and casual spaces?

2. Are your common areas subject to high traffic?

3. Do you often have guests?

4. What activities take place in your common areas?

5. Do you have a piano or other large piece of furniture that should be accounted for in the design of your living or family rooms?

6. Will you use a fireplace?

*If you identified as a serenity seeker:* You will prefer to keep your living room formal and separate from the casual family or rumpus room, in favor of maintaining distinctly private and public areas of the home.

*If you identified as a clever utilitarian:* Your biggest consideration will be to ensure that there is sufficient and appropriately appointed space for each activity that occurs within the common areas of your home.

*If you identified as a sophisticated entertainer:* Depending on the types of events you host at your home, you might prefer open, great room areas. You should consider an energy-efficient, gas-burning, timer or remote-controlled fireplace for the ambiance and convenience. If members of your household work or study within your common areas, you'll want to take that into account during the design phase of your project so that there is appropriate wiring for computers or a built-in desk.

## WORK AREA

1. Do you work from home?

2. Do you work primarily on a laptop or desktop?

3. Do you have lots of office equipment, or just a laptop and a small printer?

4. Do you handle, store, or discard lots of paperwork?

5. Will this office be for your exclusive use, shared by other adults, or shared by adults and children alike?

6. Do you need upgraded electrical wiring and additional outlets?

*If you identified as a serenity seeker:* You will keep work areas separate from bedrooms and other places that you have designated for rest and relaxation. You should attempt to maintain your own separate work area, rather than sharing it with others.

*If you identified as a clever utilitarian:* Your work area will be meticulous and private. Family members or housemates will likely have their own workspace elsewhere in the home. Your work areas will include functional desks and space for storing paperwork.

*If you identified as a sophisticated entertainer:* Your office will be high-tech and highly functional. You will likely have a wireless network that connects multiple computers in the home as well as fax machines and printers. Your office furniture will be constructed to artfully display your top-of-the-line office equipment. Keeping clutter at bay is important to you, so a paper shredder is a must-have.

## EXTERIOR AREAS

1. Do you garden?

2. How much time, on average, do you spend maintaining your yard or is it professionally maintained?

3. Do you have an irrigation system?

4. Is the area subject to hot or cold extremes?

5. Does it rain or snow frequently?

6. Do you entertain outdoors? If so, how often?

7. How many cars do you own?

8. Do you use the garage as a work or exercise area?

*If you identified as a serenity seeker:* You could go either way with your landscaping, depending on whether you enjoy gardening or lush landscaping. If you enjoy the look, but not the feel, of mature gardens you might hire a landscaper to periodically maintain your yard. If you like a more southwestern feel, you're in luck. Many southwestern plants grow beautifully for years with little to no maintenance. A garage that allows you to pull in to your sanctuary and close out the busy world is likely to be high on your list of must-haves.

*If you identified as a clever utilitarian:* You might consider a garage with all the organizational and storage bells and whistles, including hooks for hockey sticks and bicycles, space for your cars, and perhaps even a workbench. With respect to your yard, if you are a gardener, you might like a potting bench or some similar dedicated space to store and use your gardening tools and materials.

*If you identified as a sophisticated entertainer:* You may want a garage that features a coated, oil-resistant, stone-look concrete coating. In your outdoor spaces, you should consider a granite-topped outdoor kitchen, or an outdoor fireplace and seating area for you to entertain your guests. If you live in a snowy climate, heated sidewalks can minimize the effort involved in keeping your sidewalks safe for you and your visitors.

## Your Property and Your Profile

Cleary, two trillion dollar women with different profiles can remodel their kitchens with entirely distinct, but equally pleasing, results. Hopefully, you now have some life-enhancing ideas for your remodeling projects or new home finishes. Taking the time to align your property plans with your profile can make the difference between giving your home life a facelift and changing the way you experience life.

# CHAPTER 7

# Condo Can-Do

## Tips, Tools, and Secrets for Buying a New Condominium or Remodeling Your Unit

I've found that the higher maintenance your lifestyle is the lower maintenance you might want your home to be. This might explain why über-busy women such as Gwyneth Paltrow, Jennifer Lopez, and even Oprah all own condos! Women all over America are opting out of mowing lawns, upgrading roofs, and fixing burst pipes and opting into the condo (or townhouse, coop, or loft) lifestyle, whether they live solo or have kids, husbands, and dogs! In fact, the National Association of Realtors reported that 42% of condo buyers were single women in 2006.

## What Is a Condo?

Technically, the term *condominium* refers to the legal form of ownership in which each unit's owner owns the four interior walls and the air between the units and a parking space. The units' owners also share ownership of portions of the property or *common area*. Most often, the common area includes

- plumbing and wiring
- exterior walls
- roofs

**113**

- hallways and outdoor walkways
- common streets, parking lots, and ground
- recreational areas

However, most people use the word *condo* as shorthand for the actual units within a multifamily building, complex, or development. Townhomes and flats are the two flavors of condos. Townhomes have two or more floors in each unit, and flats are units that can be stacked on top of each other in a multistory building.

Living in a condo entails living in close proximity to your neighbors and being jointly responsible for the maintenance of the commonly owned areas. This communal aspect of condo living has tangible benefits, but there are also disadvantages. Condo living can be a noisy existence. You might share walls with someone who has a huge going-away party the night before your big presentation. Is your building sufficiently soundproofed to allow you to sleep like a baby through the swinging soiree next door? It's your job to ask.

The advantages of condo living are many. For starters, you never actually have to maintain your yard or the building. Your monthly home owner's association (HOA) dues pay for regular maintenance inside and outside your building. Your dues also afford you access to onsite amenities and services such as fitness centers, pools and spas, business facilities, greenbelts or private parks, clubhouses, parking garages, doormen—and the list goes on!

One of the latest trends in new, urban condo buildings is to locate a full-sized upscale grocery store, such as Whole Foods Market, and a full-sized health club on the ground floor—then build condos on top, and give condo owners memberships to the gym as part of the deed to their unit.

Clearly, owning a condo creates a number of unique opportunities for a sophisticated, single lifestyle or even a family life without some of the hassles of maintaining a detached house. Similarly, buying a new condo, townhome, co-op, or loft presents some unique decisions to be made; and remodeling these units must be done with consideration for your community, not just your family.

# Buying a Newly Built Condo

If you have decided to go for the lower-maintenance home life that a condo or townhome offers, and you plan to purchase a unit in a brand-new building or complex, you might also have unwittingly streamlined your entire new home buying process. Once you have selected your community, there are fewer decisions you will need to make than if you had purchased a new detached home. However, there are a few items that are of particular concern when you are purchasing a condo.

## Location, Location, Location

Clearly, the location of your condo community is critical. However, the location of your unit within the building and within the community overall (if your community has more than one building) is even more important. The advantage of buying in a new building or complex is that you will have the opportunity to pick a great location. However, because the complex or building may not be occupied or even fully built, you may not be able to get a true sense of the noise level where your unit is located.

Deciding between higher and lower floors is one of the quintessential dilemmas for condo buyers. Clearly, the top floor is desirable because you won't hear footsteps, running water, or other noise from people who live above you. If your building is appropriately soundproofed, as most new buildings are, you should not be able to hear footsteps and running water on lower floors. Residents on higher floors experience more difficulty transporting items to their unit. This is especially true when you are moving in, redecorating, remodeling, and even just bringing your groceries in. If your building has an elevator, living on higher floors may not present as much of a logistical challenge. Many women prefer ground floor units for ease of access—you never have to take the stairs and you never have to wait for the elevator. Single women buyers often opt for higher floors for security reasons.

### End unit or middle unit

End units are located on the corners of a building. Most people love end units because they have more windows and light than the average unit, fewer neighbors, and presumably, less noise. Because these units are so desirable, condo developers often charge a premium for them. However, it can be worth it to pay the premium in exchange for the enhanced resale value of the unit.

### Proximity to community amenities

Before you select your unit, get a sense for where it is relative to the following services or centers in your building or complex. Having a unit that is close to the garage or parking lot is nice for ease of access to and from your vehicle, but there are downsides such as exhaust, noise, and foot traffic.

If you use the recreational or fitness facilities with regularity, it might be nice to live close on those days when your motivation is running low. However, if you are considering buying a unit that is across from the pool or clubhouse, consider the noise level. What will the pool look like—and sound like—when kids are out of school? What about when someone throws a party at the clubhouse?

Many communities have business centers, which don't tend to be particularly noisy. As such, if you plan to use the business center, being nearby can be a real positive, without much downside.

It can be convenient to live near the elevator. However, most of your neighbors will have to pass your unit, which can get noisy. The sound of the elevator itself and the arrival bell might be a problem if you had to hear it hundreds of times a day. Depending on your unit's soundproofing and how much time you spend at home, this may or may not be a problem.

If possible, choose a unit that is far away from the loading dock. Loading docks are notoriously noisy. Imagine the daily 5:00 a.m. cacophony of beep-beep-beeps that trucks make when they back in to unload. Loading docks are mostly found in larger buildings, and most builders are pretty strategic about their placement in order to impact as few units as possible.

## Options and Upgrades

Chapter 4 details how to position yourself to make conscious and reasoned options and upgrades selections. The same information applies with condos. However, when you're buying a condo, there can be a greater temptation to break the bank because the upgrades may not be quite as expensive as they would be in a home. As such, if you plan to eventually sell your unit and are at all concerned about recouping some of the outlay you made for upgrades, be careful not to overspend!

Upgrades will drive up your purchase price, which will in turn cause you to overprice your home when you resell it. It is important to know that the top three demographic categories who buy condos are single women, first time home buyers, and retirees looking to downsize. All three of these groups can be price-sensitive. If you put your home on the market and there are identical units listed at a significantly lower price, your unit might be left sitting on the market or you might have to sell it for a much lower price. If you're unit is in an upscale complex where all the units are likely to be highly upgraded or if you just are not concerned about recouping the cost of your upgrades, don't worry about this. But if you are the average trillion dollar woman, you might want to stay in the mid-range with your finish materials, rather than breaking the bank to replicate the Taj Mahal.

## Nearly New? Condo Conversions

There is a stunning array of beautifully remodeled, condo conversion units available for sale all over the country at incredible prices. In some ways, these units are similar to new condos. The seller is a builder/developer, so you may be able to choose from a number of units, and you may even be able to make choices of your finish materials, including granite for the counters, floor and window coverings, and more.

Condo conversion units and grounds may look new, but they are not new buildings. They are former apartment buildings that have undergone a thorough renovation to be sold individually as condos. You are likely to get a one-year home warranty, rather than the 10-year builder's warranty you would get with most new units. Also, there may be defects or malfunctioning systems in a conversion unit that you just can't see with the naked eye.

When I represent buyers of condo conversion units, I schedule a professional home inspector to inspect the units. The inspector does an intense walk-through inspection of the unit and tests the HVAC system, water faucets, toilets, and electrical outlets and points out issues, deficiencies, and any areas that might warrant repairs. Within one or two business days, your inspector will issue you a written report describing the systems contained within your unit and listing any repairs that need to be made.

Condo conversion developers vary widely, but I have worked with some who respond promptly to a request for repairs and send their crew out to fix the items called for by the inspector. You can find a certified home inspector online by visiting the American Society of Home Inspectors Web site (www.ashi.org) or the National Association of Certified Home Inspectors Web site (www.nachi.org).

## HOA Disclosures

When you buy a condominium or a unit in a coop, you are creating a legal relationship with the other owners in the community. The terms of that relationship are spelled out in the HOA disclosures. This set of documents usually consists of the following:

- *bylaws:* the legal documents that create the HOA, define its authority, create its board of directors, and set forth the basic obligations and rights of HOA members (owners of the units)
- *accounting information:* a budget (itemizing revenue from HOA dues and expenses for the maintenance of various common areas, insurance, and property management) and a reserve statement (stating how much money the builder is putting in a reserve account for the HOA)
- *covenants, conditions, and restrictions (CC&Rs):* a contract between the association members that states they agree to cer-

tain limitations on how the homes and common areas may be used and altered

- *rules and regulations:* a list of hours of operation for the pool and dates and times for garbage collection, among other things
- *board meeting minutes:* an account of the HOA's board of directors meetings
- *newsletters:* a community communication tool that provides weekly or monthly information about community events

Read these disclosures in their entirety. You can't know what the plan is or what your duties and rights are without reading these documents. The CC&Rs may include restrictions on where you can park, what you can do to your unit, and how you can use the facilities. You need to be sure that you agree with these restrictions before you buy the condo.

Make sure you understand when the builder will transfer the HOA operations to the community. Because the builder or developer created the community, state laws require the builder or developer to create and manage the HOA until it can operate independently.

### Understand all of the costs upfront

Depending on how your HOA is set up, in addition to your monthly dues, you may have to pay regular or special assessment fees for using certain community facilities. You may also have to pay penalty fees for violating community rules. Some communities require that you purchase your Internet and cable services through the HOA. You need to know all the costs of owning and living in the community, whether the costs are subject to change, and the process involved in changing costs before you buy into the community.

### Understand your insurance policy

When you own a home, your home owner's insurance policy covers both the building and the personal property inside the building, such as furniture, computers, clothes, etc. When you buy a condo, though, the insurance protection provided by your HOA only protects the struc-

## Trillion Dollar Tip #11

### HOA dues = costs of ownership, consolidated

I have known home buyers who were as allergic to HOA dues as I am to cats. I have literally had people who would love to live in an HOA-run community refuse to do so because they thought they would be paying hundreds of dollars a month simply for the privilege of living there.

When you pay dues to the HOA, you pay for:

- your home owner's insurance (the HOA obtains a policy that covers the whole building and just charges you for your share)
- common area maintenance (landscaping, cleaning, repairs and improvements, and garbage removal)
- gas (most often, if gas lines are shared between units)
- water (often, as plumbing is often shared between units)

Some HOA dues include access to recreational facilities such as the golf course or health club, whereas others include building concierge and doorman services. Your HOA disclosures from the builder will itemize all the costs covered by your dues.

On the positive side, you'll write fewer checks monthly, as HOA dues cover many costs you would have to pay on your own in a detached home. Also, lots of unexpected repair costs are liable to be covered by your HOA. Between the HOA and your builder's warranty, you can dramatically reduce your risk of big repair costs. Access to onsite recreational and convenience amenities can be a big savings—if you use them.

Conversely, your dues might be more expensive than the total of your water, gas, maintenance, and insurance costs would be otherwise. The overage usually goes to pay the management company and to create a reserve fund for repairs and maintenance.

ture—not the contents of your home. Make sure you get an insurance policy to protect the contents of your home, similar to a renter's insurance policy, to protect against theft or disaster. Contents policies are quite inexpensive and can prevent you from losing everything you own other than your home. Not sure who to call? Ask your mortgage broker for a referral or call your car insurance company—they often provide multiple policy discounts.

### Get actively involved early in the game

Some HOAs are very amiable, others are full of conflict, and others function well without much person-to-person involvement. Because your new HOA may not have any group dynamics issues yet—good or bad—you are in a perfect position to help create them have. Go to the meetings, participate, and seek a seat on the board if you have time. At the very least, read the board meeting minutes and newsletters regularly so that you can stay actively informed.

# Remodeling a Condo Unit—By the Bylaws

If you already own a condo, you know that there are two types of HOA members: those that abide by the rules and those that are in constant conflict with their neighbors because they refuse to abide by the rules. You are a trillion dollar woman, so chances are that you are the former. What you may not know, or remember, when you bought your unit is that your HOA documents may actually contain guidelines for what you can and cannot do to your unit.

If you are planning a remodel, before you run to the bookstore to grab the latest issue of *Architectural Digest* or *Elle Décor* for inspiration, you should go to your home buying file and grab your CC&Rs and read the architectural and remodeling guidelines, before you get your heart set on doing something that might violate the rules. You should review these guidelines before you develop your full-fledged vision of home for your remodel. If you don't, you run the risk of falling in love with your plan, only to find out later (maybe even thousands of dollars later) that it cannot be done.

## You're Not the Boss of Me!

Most HOA guidelines set forth the following:

■ the specific remodeling projects that require HOA approval

- the process for seeking HOA approval, usually involving submission of plans to the architectural committee or board of directors for review
- the guidelines that some common projects must meet in order to successfully receive HOA approval

Many home owners have wondered why on earth the HOA has the right to impose guidelines or restrictions on what they can and can't do to their units. If you live in a community of attached—or even some detached homes—your neighbors could be affected by your remodel. And I'm talking about more than just the noise of hammers for a couple of weeks; your contractor could cause their plumbing to leak, your changes to your balcony could impact their view, and your replacement of plush carpet with hardwood floors can exponentially increase the sound of your footsteps for your downstairs neighbors. In general, HOA remodeling guidelines exist to minimize the impact your project will have on your neighbors.

## The Golden Rule of Condo Remodeling

Remember the Golden Rule: Do unto others as you would have them do unto you. If you embark upon a remodeling project without HOA approval, which adversely impacts your neighbors or otherwise violates the HOA rules, you can be forced to stop work or even remove the new features that were installed. To avoid this costly mistake, you should seek HOA approval even if your remodeling project does not fall within the architectural restrictions of your HOA.

For example, if your remodel will impact the plumbing, wiring, gas lines, or framing in the walls between units, you should get approval from your HOA before starting your project. If there is any conceivable reason that your neighbor(s) might complain about your project after it is done, you can rest assured that they will. You can avoid this unnecessary drama by simply getting approval in the first place. The HOA might require you to change your plans to minimize the impact on your neighbors. Think about it: Wouldn't you prefer to make a change rather than have to rip out your $3,000 jetted bathtub after installation because the vibration cracked the ceiling in the unit below?

## Common Condo Remodeling Restrictions

The approval process should be set forth in your HOA documents. Most likely, it will require you to submit your written plans, along with details about your contractor, insurance policies, and plans to seal the unit. The architectural committee will review your application and suggest any necessary revisions. If the work is structurally intensive, the HOA might require a structural engineer to sign off on the plans. After you receive approval, you should proceed to obtain city approval and permits. Your HOA might choose to periodically inspect the work to ensure that it is being completed according to plans. There are a number of remodeling plans that are highly likely to require approval.

### Installing hard flooring if your unit is above another unit

Clearly, the noise could be an issue for your neighbor. Many HOAs have resolved this dilemma by implementing guidelines for sound-buffering materials that must be installed under the flooring. Your HOA may require approval of this sort of project to ensure that your flooring will comply with soundproofing requirements.

### Installing new windows or screen doors

If your HOA does not handle window replacement, it will probably have a few options for acceptable replacement windows. Similarly, if you want to install screen doors, the HOA might regulate the look and feel of acceptable screens—even down to the brand name and color. This is just to ensure uniformity, so that one unit doesn't end up with rainbow polka dots on its windows or screen doors.

### Projects impacting commonly owned areas

Any project that involves framing, electrical wiring, gas and plumbing lines within the common walls, floors or shared ceilings will likely require HOA approval. Also, anything that affects common air ducts and cable or telephone wires or requires even temporary utility shut-downs will require HOA approval.

### Balcony enclosures

Building walls or adding a sunroom enclosure to your balcony can add sufficient weight to its structural soundness and can also be less-than-attractive from the exterior. Your HOA will likely need to sign off on any such project.

### Moving interior walls

If the walls being moved are non-weight bearing (they don't support any of the structure), your HOA will probably quickly approve your project. However, if the walls to be moved are structural walls, the HOA may require you to provide engineered plans, just as the city would.

In addition to regulating the types of projects that you can or can't do, your HOA may also regulate some of the logistics of your remodeling project.

### Work hours

For example, your HOA may require your remodeling work to occur Monday through Saturday, 8:30 a.m. to 5:00 p.m. in order to minimize the disruption to other residents.

### Contractor

Your HOA may need to approve your contractor. They will likely just want to review their licensure and make sure that they agree to building rules. Depending on the scope of the project, the HOA may also require that the contractor agree to cover the building for liability created by any of the contractor's work; a really small contractor may not be able to do this.

### Insurance

Your HOA may require that you and/or your contractor obtain insurance policies that name the building and the HOA as additional insured parties. For elevator, parking, or debris removal, the HOA might impose regulations on your contractors' use of the passenger elevators, where they can park, and where they can store debris containers. Many HOAs also require that you seal your unit during the project to prevent dust, odors, and fumes from passing into neighboring units.

It may seem than your HOA remodeling committee is more high maintenance than your actual unit. But it is worth the work to comply with the rules to maintain your relationships with your neighbors. If your project is small in scope or complies with the written guidelines, the approval process can be a breeze. Minor projects such as painting, cabinet replacement, conventional appliance replacement, changing lights, bathroom and kitchen fixtures, and changing carpeting do not normally require HOA approval. However, you should contact your HOA office to see if there are any limitations (such as work hours) on these types of projects.

## Keep it Drama Free

Once your unit is ready to remodel, keep your life as drama free as possible by complying with your HOA's remodeling regulations and keeping your plans as neighbor friendly as possible. Living in close quarters can be a benefit, if you protect your relationships with your neighbors.

# CHAPTER 8

# Your Green House

## Creating an Eco-Friendly Home

**W**omen are the stewards of the earth. We have a track record of going the extra mile to care for the earth and its resources. Authors Kira Gould and Lance Hosey argue that women are the "greener gender." In *Women in Green: Voices in Sustainable Design*, the authors suggest that

- Women are up to 15% more likely than men to rank the environment as a high priority.
- Women make up 66% of voters who vote on issues with environmental impact.
- Women are more likely than men to donate their money and volunteer their time to environmental causes; especially when those causes are connected to the health and safety of their local community.

Women are especially prolific on issues of environmentally responsible construction and design. Since the dawn of the green and sustainable building phenomenon, many of the leading architects, designers, activists, and politicians have been women—despite the fact that women are a stark minority in the architecture and construction fields.

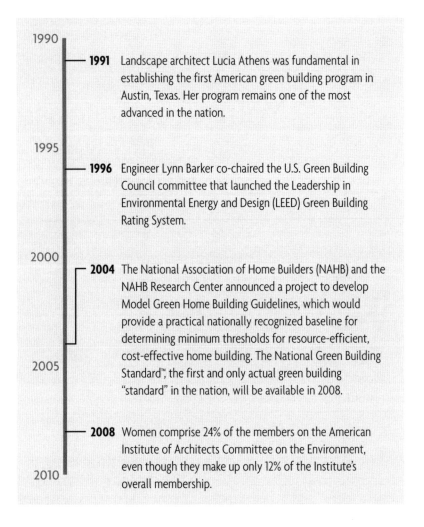

1990

— **1991**  Landscape architect Lucia Athens was fundamental in establishing the first American green building program in Austin, Texas. Her program remains one of the most advanced in the nation.

1995

— **1996**  Engineer Lynn Barker co-chaired the U.S. Green Building Council committee that launched the Leadership in Environmental Energy and Design (LEED) Green Building Rating System.

2000

— **2004**  The National Association of Home Builders (NAHB) and the NAHB Research Center announced a project to develop Model Green Home Building Guidelines, which would provide a practical nationally recognized baseline for determining minimum thresholds for resource-efficient, cost-effective home building. The National Green Building Standard™, the first and only actual green building "standard" in the nation, will be available in 2008.

2005

— **2008**  Women comprise 24% of the members on the American Institute of Architects Committee on the Environment, even though they make up only 12% of the Institute's overall membership.

2010

## Why Women Care About Green Living

Speaking from a Darwinian, survival-of-the-species perspective, women take on responsibility for the health and safety of their families. In our world, this means doing what we can to ensure the availability of clean and abundant water, air, food, and energy for generations to come. This sense of responsibility that women feel for the world of the future translates into their tendency to listen to the alarm bells in the news that are alerting us to environmental crisis after environmental crisis and to respond proactively by choosing to make our homes green.

Depending on where you're coming from philosophically, the word *green* may have very different connotations. Some people automatically think granola and Birkenstocks; whereas others think of green living as being thoughtful of the environment as they move through their daily lives. When green is attached to building, remodeling, or living, it simply implies doing those things with a conscious awareness of the impact our actions have on the environment and being responsible in our use of the earth's resources.

## What is Green Building?

Green building simply applies this mindfulness to the art and science of architecture, design, and construction. Generally speaking, there are four elements of green building. Green homes are environmentally responsible and ecologically sustainable in the way they are (1) located, (2) designed, (3) built, and (4) operated.

According to the NAHB, a home can be considered green when energy efficiency, water and resource conservation, the use of sustainable or recycled products, and indoor air quality considerations are incorporated into the process of home building.

The increased availability of education for builders, growing consumer awareness, and the exploding market for sustainable, environmentally friendly and recycled building products has accelerated green building's acceptance rate and move into the mainstream.

Today, more than half of NAHB's members, who build 85% of the homes in this country, will be incorporating green practices into the development, design, and construction of new homes by the end of 2007. The graphic, *How Homes Become Green,* is a visual sampling of the innovations in materials, appliances, and techniques that can turn a home green.

Even if you don't incorporate major renovations or new building technologies to "green up" your home, there are tons of ways you can operate your home in an environmentally sound manner.

## ENERGY INNOVATION
# How Homes Become Green

More durable roof coverings such as steel and fiber cement reduce the frequency of roof replacement. Lighter colors absorb less heat, reducing cooling costs in warm climates. Now, solar roofing products integrate asphalt shingles, standing-seam metal roofing, and slate or concrete tiles.

Oriented strand board (OSB) is an engineered wood product that does not require large trees for its manufacture. It is resource efficient and enhances durability and is used to sheathe roofs and walls in 75 percent of new homes.

Tree preservation reduces landscaping and future energy costs and helps provide winter wind breaks or summer shade. Additional landscaping improves the environment even more: One tree can filter 60 lbs. of pollutants from the air each year.

New toilets have redesigned bowls and tanks that use less water, but function more efficiently than rst-generation low-flow models. Some use pumps for supplementary water pressure. Advanced shower and sink faucet aerators provide the same flow regardless of pressure to reduce water use and the energy required to heat it.

Energy-efficient windows incorporating advanced technologies like low-emittance (low-E) glass coatings, gas filler between layers, and composite framing materials keep heat inside in the winter and outside in the summer.

Recycled plastic lumber and wood composite materials reduce reliance on chemically treated lumber and durable hardwood for decks, porches, trim and fencing.

Vinyl siding on exterior walls saves money on installation and maintenance; fiber-cement siding is termite- and water-resistant and warrantied to last 50 years.

Increasing the amount and R-value of insulation is a cost-effective way to save energy and help reduce heating and cooling bills, which account for at least half of energy use in the home. Sprayed insulation made of foam, cellulose or wool is an alternative to traditional glass fiber batting.

The energy efficiency of refrigerators and freezers has tripled over the last three decades because they have more insulation, advanced compressors, better door seals and more accurate temperature controls. Front-loading washers use about 40% less water and half the energy of conventional models. Energy Star®-rated appliances save an average of 30 percent over standard models.

Incorporating passive solar design features like large, south-facing windows helps heat the home in the winter and allows for increased natural daylighting.

Covered entries at exterior doors help to prevent water intrusion, reducing maintenance and enhancing durability.

Factory-built components including trusses and pre-hung doors allow more efficient use of raw materials, making the most out of every piece of lumber. These products eliminate the need to cut wood at the jobsite, further reducing waste.

Xeriscaping, or using native plants, significantly reduces the need for watering, fertilizers and herbicides.

Selecting more efficient, correctly sized heating, cooling and water-heating equipment saves money. Tankless water heaters provide hot water on demand at a preset temperature rather than storing it, which reduces or eliminates standby losses. Geothermal heat pumps work with the Earthis renewable energy and can also heat water.

Foundations should be as well insulated as the living space walls for efficient home energy use and enhanced comfort, particularly if the basement is used as a family room or bedroom.

In addition to natural wood, flooring choices include low-VOC (volatile organic compounds) carpets for better indoor air quality, laminates that successfully mimic scarce hardwood, and linoleum, a natural product making a design comeback.

Source: National Association of Home Builders
Illustration: Rick Vitullo

## Benefits of a Green Home

Many green lifestyle proponents are motivated primarily by the idea of doing their part to encourage a healthy planet. If you are a little less altruistic or just interested to know why else a green home is worth the effort, consider some of these benefits of running a green home:

- *financial benefits:* Because green homes use less energy and water, you can expect your utility bills to be as much as 65% lower!

- *energy efficient:* Because of their location and design, green homes tend to be cooler in the summer and warmer in the winter. Energy efficient insulation, appliances, lighting, and construction can minimize drafts and keep temperatures comfortable with minimal energy use.

- *health benefits:* Green home builders avoid the use of paints, finishes, countertops, furniture, cabinetry, and carpeting that emit indoor pollution. Many particle board products give off formaldehyde, and many paints, solvents, and carpets emit volatile organic compounds (VOCs), which are low-level toxic indoors, but evolve into greenhouse gases when they escape outdoors. Reducing or eliminating these items can drastically diminish asthma-type and respiratory symptoms.

- *aesthetic benefits:* Many green living products and materials are simply beautiful to look at. It is as though their designers put as much or more thought into their appearance as they did into their efficiency and sustainability.

- *home maintenance benefits:* Similarly, many green building products not only include reused or recycled materials, they are often more durable than their standard, non-green counterpart materials and require less maintenance. For example, Trex, a popular decking material made from recycled plastics and waste wood, looks like wood but does not splinter or rot.

Some trillion dollar women have the misconception that green living involves living in a yurt, log cabin, or geodesic dome in a field somewhere. However, it is completely possible to live green and live chic. Green-built homes are some of the most gorgeous buildings you'll find on the new home market, and many push the envelope of design in a very contemporary and aesthetically artful manner. You'll also find that many of the home furnishings made for green living are created with an eye for aesthetics, often more so than their standard, non-green parallel products.

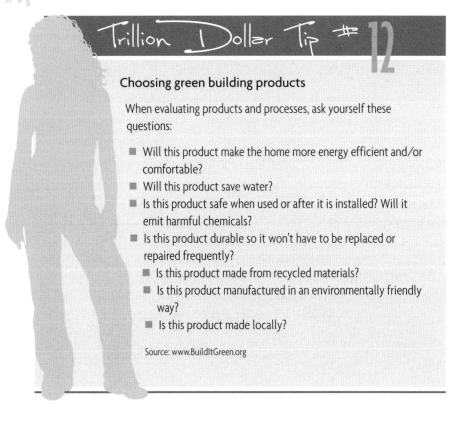

## Trillion Dollar Tip #12

### Choosing green building products

When evaluating products and processes, ask yourself these questions:

- Will this product make the home more energy efficient and/or comfortable?
- Will this product save water?
- Is this product safe when used or after it is installed? Will it emit harmful chemicals?
- Is this product durable so it won't have to be replaced or repaired frequently?
- Is this product made from recycled materials?
- Is this product manufactured in an environmentally friendly way?
- Is this product made locally?

Source: www.BuildItGreen.org

## Buying a New Green Home

If you have been considering buying a new production home that is also green, you couldn't have selected a better time. According to the National Association of Home Builders, almost 100,000 certified green homes have been built nationwide since the mid-1990s, but more than one-third of those were built since 2004.

These numbers represent homes that were built under several locally governed green building certification programs nationwide; many other green homes are built without participating in any such program. As such, this data only reflects a portion of the homes that were actually built using green technologies.

Although 100,000 green homes is an impressive and important milestone, it is still just a tiny fraction of homes built nationwide every year. Many cities and states have few or no true green home subdivisions or developments, so if there is nothing available in your area, or the green homes being built don't meet your other lifestyle needs, you might feel as though your new home can't be a green one.

However, there are degrees of green building, and most new homes will be inherently green to some extent. There are many green technologies, like energy-efficient insulation, windows, appliances, and home systems that are now standard in new construction across the board. There is a second level of even greener items (like tankless water heaters, low-VOC paints, and bamboo flooring) that are available in many new home developments as options or upgrades. And finally, there is the final level of green to which your home can only get if you operate it as a green home once you move in. You control that entirely, and only you can implement green living measures at home, no matter how green or standard your home was built.

There are several things you can do when selecting your home that can make your home life greener, even if your home itself is built with standard building materials and practices:

- Choose a new home community that is located within a short walk or commute to your job, schools, and the places you spend your free time.
- Select a home that is the right size for your family, and think to the future. If you have an overly large house, you will need to heat and cool the entire home. If your house is too small, you will overwork its systems and appliances.
- If possible pick a lot or situate your house so that most windows will face south. Southern exposure lets in light, without letting in much heat. West-facing windows provide too much heat.
- When selecting your flooring, use as much hard flooring and as little carpeting as possible. In addition to being a magnet for dust mites, mold, and allergens, carpet emits VOCs.
- Install energy efficient appliances. In most areas, your local utility will actually give you a rebate for making such a wise choice.

If you are buying a new production home, your options for green building are somewhat limited by the options available to you in the community you select. But if you are remodeling your home, you can go as green (or as light green) as you want and can afford to.

## Selecting a Green Contractor or Design Professional

Austin Energy's Green Building Program is the oldest and perhaps most well-developed municipal green building program in the country. When it comes to selecting a green contractor or designer for your remodeling project they recommend that you ask your contractor the following questions.

- ■ *Does the professional have a green philosophy of building?* Do they understand how building practices relate to the broader environment? Do they care about how our use of resources will affect the world we leave for our children? Are they trying to give you the "right" answers just to get your money, or do they demonstrate real commitment to the health of the planet?

- ■ *Does the professional demonstrate a general knowledge of green building?* If you ask about low-VOC paints, non-ozone-depleting insulation, heating and cooling design by Manual J, composting, sealed-combustion appliances, passive solar design and just get a blank stare, chances are this person is not a green building professional. Be sure to do your homework on these topics first. *Profit from Building Green* (BuilderBooks.com®) is a good read to familiarize yourself with energy-efficient building techniques.

- ■ *If you are interested in an unconventional material or technique, does the professional have the expertise and experience to provide you with it?* You might be interested in a rainwater collection system or an earth-sheltered house. If no one in the area has done what you want, can this professional demonstrate the ability to accomplish something out of the ordinary?

- *Does the professional stay abreast of advances in green building?* Do they attend local, state, or national green building program seminars and conferences? Do they read major publications such as *Environmental Building News*? Are they familiar with innovative local green building projects? Does the contractor know who in the area is doing various kinds of green building?

- *Does the professional understand the importance of a team approach in producing a green home?* A building is a system—all parts affect all other parts. Does the contractor view the designer, trade contractors and you, the client, as equally important players on the same team, all working together to bring into being a high-quality home where you can be happy, comfortable, and productive?

- *Is the professional proud of his/her work?* Is this builder glad to have you call on former clients and visit completed projects? What green measures have they included in their past projects? What are they recommending for your particular project? How much will the building exceed any recognized standards? Can they provide any warranties?

In terms of costs, Austin Energy offers this sage advice:

> Do not be deterred from building green because you are afraid you can't afford it. It's true that some green building options cost more than the standard alternative, but some of the most environmentally friendly buildings available are among the least costly. It pays to be a knowledgeable buyer, and as in many other purchases we make in our lives, you also often get what you pay for. A good green builder or designer has a real understanding of what truly makes a more environmentally-friendly building and knows precisely what to specify to get it.
>
> If a desirable option costs more upfront, take the longest view you can. Examine how it would actually affect your monthly mortgage payment. Think about how often you might have to repair or replace this item. If the item has implications for occupant health, consider this seriously, even if you can't put a precise dollar figure on it initially.

## Elements of a Green Home—Room by Room

Whether you are building or remodeling, if you want to live green at home without sacrificing style or comfort, there is a green building material you could select or a green strategy you could implement in every room in your home. This room-by-room guide details the many things you can do to make your home and lifestyle as earth friendly as possible.

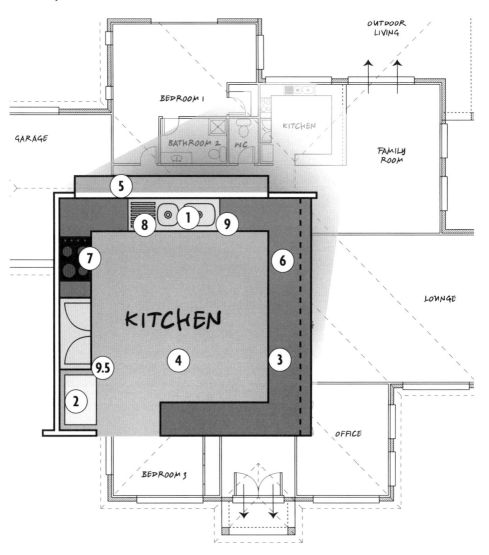

# 9.5 Strategies for a Green Kitchen

1. Install a built-in recycling and/or composting center near or under the sink.

2. The kitchen is the biggest energy drain in the house, due mostly to oversized and underutilized appliances. If you are a household of restaurant diners, don't get a huge refrigerator. If you are single, don't run the dishwasher with two forks, a cup and a plate in it—wait until it's full! Install an energy efficient dishwasher and refrigerator.

3. Use natural and low-emission cabinetry, countertops, and flooring in your new kitchen. Materials like particle board (the base of many manufactured cabinets and older countertops, and the material upon which many linoleum floors were installed) emit formaldehyde for life. They emit even more formaldehyde when they are near a heat source. Use solid, sustainable wood cabinets; tile or wood floors; and granite, stone, or tile countertops to eliminate these toxic fumes.

4. Choose low maintenance surfaces and floors that are easy to clean without harsh, environmentally harmful chemicals such as ammonia or bleach.

5. Many kitchens are poorly lit. If you're remodeling, consider enlarging the windows to let light in and reduce your dependence on electric lights. Also, locate your countertop workspaces near the windows to shed a little natural light on your cooking.

6. Use natural or low-VOC cabinet finishes and tile grout.

7. Don't forget ventilation. The air quality in the kitchen can be the worst in the entire house due to smoke, cooking odors, and fumes. Include an energy-efficient hood or countertop ventilation system in your remodeling plans.

8. Recycle and reuse as often as possible. Rinse and reuse zipper sandwich bags. Avoid using plastic grocery bags and buy reusable canvas bags instead. If you've always coveted old farmhouse kitchen cabinets, go get some, from the old farmhouse. Check out architectural salvage depots for kitchen cabinets and countertops.

9. Make sure your cleaners are greener, too. Use non-toxic, organic kitchen cleaning products, hand soaps, and dishwashing detergents.

9.5 Stock your kitchen with fresh produce and wares from your local farmer's market. By doing so, you support a local farmer and reduce the emissions the big stores create by transporting food across the country. Plus, your food will be fresher, tastier, and retain more of its nutrition.

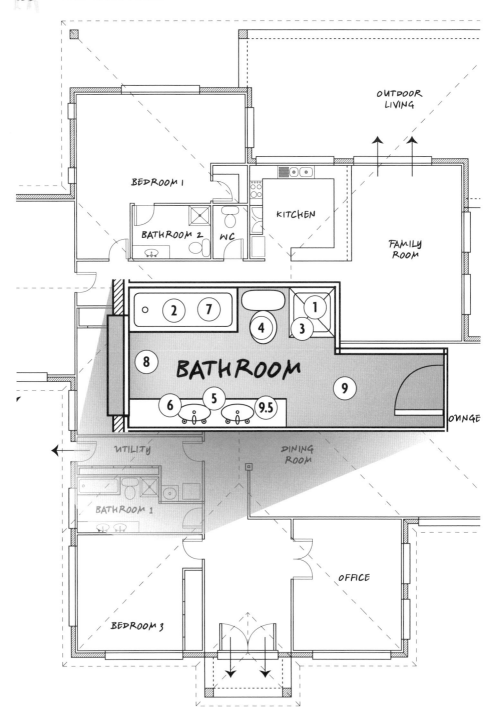

# 9.5 Strategies for Green Bathrooms

1. Replace your showerheads with low-flow options, and install showerhead shutoff valves in your showers. By doing so, you can reduce the water flow while you lather your hair or body at the flick of a finger, and save thousands of gallons of water every year.

2. If you are replacing your shower, tub, or sink, consider using vintage or reclaimed pieces from an architectural salvage depot. Every girl loves a clawfoot tub; just make sure you retrofit yours with low-flow faucets and showerheads.

3. Tile is always preferable to fiberglass or acrylic when it comes to surfacing shower walls and floors. Tile is very durable, whereas fiberglass shower stalls are difficult to repair if damaged.

4. Your toilet uses about 28% of the water in your house. When you apply for your permits, most cities will require you to replace old toilets with low-flow toilets that cut water usage in half. A low-flow toilet pays for itself in six years, in terms of water cost savings. If you don't think the low-flush toilets, ahem, do the job all the time, consider dual flush toilets. These toilets have flushers marked 1 and 2 for flushing when you do a #1 or #2. The #1 button uses just a tiny bit of water, and the #2 button has a little heartier flush.

5. Insulate the hot water pipes under your sink to reduce energy loss to heat transfer.

6. You've heard it a million times—don't let the water run while you brush your teeth or shave your legs. Three gallons go down the drain in the time you brush your teeth. Turn the water off until it's time to spit and rinse.

7. Take showers instead of baths—showers use about 66% less water.

8. Install effective and efficient exhaust fans in the bathroom that vent to the outside. Run the exhaust fan during and after showers. Allowing the moisture to collect on the wall and ceiling surfaces fosters mold and mildew.

9. Use simple, non-toxic cleaning and body care products. Your body absorbs about 60% of chemicals that you rub into your skin, and toxic cleaning supplies pollute our water supplies.

9.5 Fix dripping and leaking faucets and pipes immediately. Not only will you save dollars on your water bill, you'll conserve water.

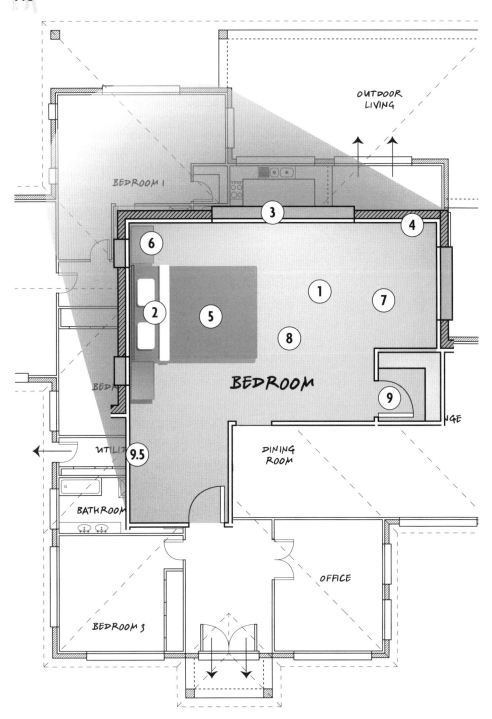

OUTDOOR
LIVING

BEDROOM 1

BEDROOM

DINING
ROOM

UTILIT

BATHROOM

BEDROOM 3

OFFICE

NGE

# 9.5 Strategies for Green Bedrooms

1.  Heating your bedroom is a no-no. The optimal room temperature for promoting sleep is 65 degrees.

2.  Enclose your pillows and mattresses in impermeable coverings, which keep out dust mites and promote healthful breathing.

3.  Minimize electric lights from streetlights, nightlights, clocks, and other electronics in your bedroom. The light disrupts the sleep hormone, melatonin.

4.  Use paints that emit low or no VOCs. Try to stick with paints containing fewer than 150 grams of VOCs per liter. If someone in your home has breathing problems, consider using vegetable- or soy-based paints.

5.  Use robes and bed linens made of organic cottons.

6.  Buy bedroom furniture made of sustainable materials, such as recycled and reclaimed woods, rather than old growth woods like mahogany.

7.  Consider radiant heating, in your bedroom and throughout the house. It is more efficient and the lack of air current blowing can alleviate respiratory problems.

8.  Install a ceiling fan to circulate warm air in the winter and cool air in the summer. Ceiling fans use much less energy than other climate control systems.

9.  If you're remodeling, build ample storage areas, closets, and cupboards. Having a place for everything ensures that everything will be in its place, which makes it more likely that you will get a good night's sleep.

9.5  Consider painting your bedroom walls serene colors like pastel blue or green. These colors can soothe away the stresses of the day and put you in a peaceful and restful state of mind.

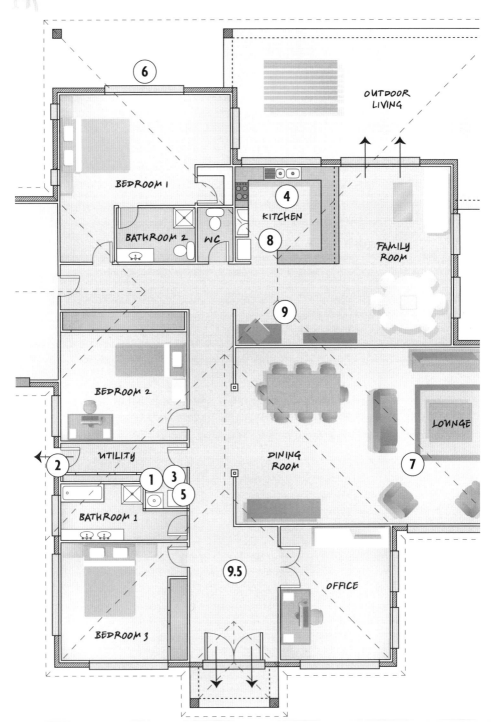

BEDROOM 1

KITCHEN

OUTDOOR LIVING

BATHROOM 2

WC

FAMILY ROOM

BEDROOM 2

DINING ROOM

LOUNGE

UTILITY

BATHROOM 1

BEDROOM 3

OFFICE

# 9.5 Strategies for House-Wide Energy Efficiency

1.  Turn your water heater down to 120 to 130 degrees. That's hot enough to kill germs, and it saves a huge amount of energy compared with the standard 140-degree setting. It also prolongs the life of your water heater. (If you're not convinced about the germ-killing deal, you should know that most new dishwashers have a temperature booster.)

2.  Insulate, insulate, insulate! Insulating your water heater and hot water pipes reduces energy usage by 5 to 10%. Also, take advantage of the opportunity a remodel presents to properly insulate walls, ductwork, and other energy drains.

3.  Consider a tankless water heater, which heats water on demand. So there's no big tank of water that needs to be heated even when it's not used, as with conventional water heaters.

4.  Use energy efficient appliances, including dishwashers, laundry machines, and refrigerators.

5.  Use pleated filters for your heating and cooling systems instead of electrostatic ones. The pleated filters cost a tenth of the price of electrostatic filters and work much better. Make sure that your filter complies with the manufacturer's recommendations.

6.  Use caulking and weather stripping to eliminate drafts and air leaks. If you are having doors or windows replaced or installed, make sure the seals are super tight.

7.  Beware of skylights! Though popular in remodels, skylights let in a lot of heat in warmer climates. Also, recessed or "canned" lighting can generate a lot of heat and draw in air from your air conditioner, forcing it to work harder. Instead, opt for tubular skylights (or lighting tubes) and sealed or air-tight recessed lighting.

8.  Make sure your appliances are the right size for your needs and that they are energy-efficient. Use the smallest appliance that can get the job done.

9.  Guard against energy vampires such as appliances, computers, televisions, microwaves, stereos, and charging adapters for laptops, PDAs, and cell phones. These items draw a phantom load of energy when they are not being used. In fact 75% of the energy they use is consumed when they are not even on! Make sure you unplug these items when not in use or plug them into a power strip.

9.5 As they burn out, replace all your standard fluorescent light bulbs with compact fluorescent bulbs. They are more expensive, but they can last up to 10 years, and they pay for themselves in about 18 months.

## The Top Ten Green Web Sites

Do you want to live, build, or remodel green? Here are some eco-friendly Web sites to get you informed and inspired.

1. *The National Association of Home Builders*
   www.nahb.org
   NAHB offers a number of resources on green building.

2. *Domino Magazine's Green Sites Directory*
   www.dominomag.com/resources/sites/greensites
   A listing of favorite eco-friendly links from the editors of *Domino Magazine*, including categories such as home furnishings, paint, flooring, and kitchen cabinetry.

3. *Energy Star*
   www.EnergyStar.gov
   Provides rankings on all sorts of building materials and appliances in accordance with EPA and Department of Energy efficiency standards.

4. *Environmental Home Center*
   www.EnvironmentalHomeCenter.com
   A comprehensive resource for green building materials, workshops, and events.

5. *IdealBite*
   www.IdealBite.com
   Free, daily, bite-sized tips for easy green living.

6. *Low Impact Living*
   www.lowimpactliving.com
   Educational resource and store for creating an environmentally sustainable home and lifestyle.

7. *Sundance Channel's The Green*
   www.SundanceChannel.com/TheGreen
   The Sundance Channel's dynamic programming block focused on green living, ecological issues, and the environment.

8. *Straw, Sticks, and Bricks*
   www.StrawSticksAndBricks.com
   Online green building materials store that allows you to buy green and help clear the air by eliminating a trip to the store.

9. *The Green Guide*

   www.TheGreenGuide.com

   Green living tips and product reviews from *National Geographic*.

   *Build It Green*

   www.builditgreen.org

10. *Green Home*

    www.GreenHome.com

    The #1 Google-rated resources for products to help you go green at home.

## Congratulations!

Yes, congratulations for working your way through the process of building the structure of knowledge with which you can move boldly into the odyssey ahead of you. Working through this book (which I hope you did) to become a trillion dollar woman can create the same feeling as when you wake up on your 21st, 30th, or 40th birthday. You don't necessarily feel any different. But a week or so later, you find yourself making a decision differently than you would have before.

So it is when you become a trillion dollar woman. You won't close this book and feel instantly qualified to go out and single-handedly build a house. However, when it comes time to meet with your real estate agent, you might feel more capable of having a conversation about what you really want and need.

You might even hear questions come out of your mouth and wonder how you knew to ask those particular questions. When your contractor prospects leave your initial interview and you pick up the call to check with past clients, you might think, "Whoa, I'm really following up." And when you walk into your design consultation with a dream book chock full of your advance wish list, prioritized by price, you might smile inwardly, knowing that you are in control of your transaction, and not vice versa.

This is the mark of the trillion dollar woman. Informed, inspired, and energized to enhance her life by buying a new home or remodeling her current home, and emboldened with sufficient knowledge to form wise questions and ask them without hesitation. So, without further ado—the time has come to start creating your Vision of Home. Good luck!

# Trillion Dollar Woman Checklists

## Home Buying Wants & Needs Checklist

Name(s): _____

Name(s) _____

Street Address: _____

City: _____ State: _____ Zip: _____

Home Phone: _____ Cell: _____

Fax: _____ ☐ Call prior to sending fax

Email Address: _____ ☐ Okay to send listings

Email Address: _____ ☐ Okay to send listings

I have decided to move because: _____

_____

I would like to move into my new home by:_____

_____

I ☐ am ☐ am not working with a mortgage broker. My mortgage broker's contact information is:

Name:_____ Phone:_____

I ☐ have ☐ have not been pre-approved for a mortgage loan up to $_____

I ☐ rent ☐ own my present home.

If renting: My monthly rent is: _____. My lease expires: _____

If owning:

I ☐ do ☐ do not need to sell my home prior to purchasing my new home.

I ☐ do ☐ do not need to refinance my home prior to purchasing my new home.

My house ☐ is ☐ is not presently on the market / in contract. (Circle one)

My house is listed with:

Agent: _____ Company: _____

Phone Number: _____ List Price: _____

The only thing(s) that would prevent me from buying a home today is:

_____

I would describe my present home as:_____

_____

What I like the most about where I live now is:_____

_____

What I like the least about where I live now is:_____

_____

In my spare time I like to:_____

_____

I would describe the home I am looking for as:_____

_____

_____

_____

I will consider living in the following cities/counties/parishes:_____

_____

I will consider (check all that apply): ☐ Condos ☐ Townhomes ☐ Single-family
☐ Co-Op ☐ Multifamily _____ # of units maximum

## The Numbers

The maximum monthly payment acceptable to me is:
$_____ per month.

I have $_____ cash available for down payment and closing costs.
I would like to use $_____ toward down payment and closing costs.

I ☐ will ☐ will not be interested in properties with HOA's.
The maximum HOA dues I can pay monthly are:

☐ Under $150  ☐ $150-250  ☐ $250-350  ☐ $350-500  ☐ $500-750  ☐ $750+

I ☐ think ☐ know I would like to look at homes in the following price range:
$_____ to $_____.

No. of bedrooms: _____ Min. _____ Preferred
No. of bathrooms: _____ Min. _____ Preferred

Square Footage (Home):
_____ Min. _____ Preferred _____ Unknown

Square Footage (Lot):
_____ Min. _____ Preferred _____ Unknown

| **LOCATION** | Must-Have | Like | Dislike | Deal-Breaker |
|---|---|---|---|---|
| Close to work (max. _____ min. commute) | ☐ | ☐ | ☐ | ☐ |
| Work address: _____ | | | | |
| _____ | | | | |
| Nearby shopping | ☐ | ☐ | ☐ | ☐ |
| City(ies):_____ | | | | |
| In school district: ☐ N/A ☐ _____(District) | ☐ | ☐ | ☐ | ☐ |

| HOME INTERIOR FEATURES | Must-Have | Like | Dislike | Deal-Breaker |
|---|---|---|---|---|
| Updated kitchen | ☐ | ☐ | ☐ | ☐ |
| Eat-in kitchen | ☐ | ☐ | ☐ | ☐ |
| Stainless steel appliances | ☐ | ☐ | ☐ | ☐ |
| Granite kitchen countertops | ☐ | ☐ | ☐ | ☐ |
| Master bedroom suite | ☐ | ☐ | ☐ | ☐ |
| Double sinks in master bath | ☐ | ☐ | ☐ | ☐ |
| Bathtub | ☐ | ☐ | ☐ | ☐ |
| Walk-in bedroom closets | ☐ | ☐ | ☐ | ☐ |
| Formal dining room | ☐ | ☐ | ☐ | ☐ |
| Formal living room | ☐ | ☐ | ☐ | ☐ |
| Family/rumpus room/den | ☐ | ☐ | ☐ | ☐ |
| Separate mud room/laundry room | ☐ | ☐ | ☐ | ☐ |
| Fireplace | ☐ | ☐ | ☐ | ☐ |
| Hardwood floors | ☐ | ☐ | ☐ | ☐ |
| Air conditioning | ☐ | ☐ | ☐ | ☐ |
| Central heat | ☐ | ☐ | ☐ | ☐ |
| CAT-5 wiring | ☐ | ☐ | ☐ | ☐ |
| Great room | ☐ | ☐ | ☐ | ☐ |
| DSL availability | ☐ | ☐ | ☐ | ☐ |
| Basement | ☐ | ☐ | ☐ | ☐ |
| High or vaulted ceilings | ☐ | ☐ | ☐ | ☐ |
| Garage: _____ car minimum; _____ car preferred | ☐ | ☐ | ☐ | ☐ |
| 2+ stories or 1 story/flat (circle one) | ☐ | ☐ | ☐ | ☐ |

| HOME EXTERIOR FEATURES | Must-Have | Like | Dislike | Deal-Breaker |
|---|---|---|---|---|
| Architectural style(s): _____ | ☐ | ☐ | ☐ | ☐ |
| Large yard/no yard to maintain (circle one) | ☐ | ☐ | ☐ | ☐ |
| Fenced front yard | ☐ | ☐ | ☐ | ☐ |
| Front yard | ☐ | ☐ | ☐ | ☐ |
| Back yard | ☐ | ☐ | ☐ | ☐ |
| Privacy from neighbors | ☐ | ☐ | ☐ | ☐ |
| Patio or deck | ☐ | ☐ | ☐ | ☐ |
| Outdoor spa/hot tub | ☐ | ☐ | ☐ | ☐ |
| Pool | ☐ | ☐ | ☐ | ☐ |
| View: _____ (describe) | ☐ | ☐ | ☐ | ☐ |

I entertain often: ☐ yes ☐ no: _____
_____

Things I can ABSOLUTELY NOT stand in my home—that I want you to never show me in a prospective property—are: _____
_____
_____

Information I will need about a prospective property before making an offer (e.g., distance to subway/bus, school buses, special educational needs, city taxes, etc.): _____
_____
_____

The five most important features I want in my home—in order of their importance:

1. _____

2. _____

3. _____

4. _____

5. _____

The following children will be living in the home being purchased:

Name: _____ Age: _____ M  F

Name: _____ Age: _____ M  F

Name: _____ Age: _____ M  F

Name: _____ Age: _____ M  F

The following pets will be living in the home being purchased:

Name: _____ Type:_____ ☐ Indoor ☐ Outdoor

Name: _____ Type:_____ ☐ Indoor ☐ Outdoor

Name: _____ Type:_____ ☐ Indoor ☐ Outdoor

Name: _____ Type:_____ ☐ Indoor ☐ Outdoor

The following number & types of vehicles will have space requirements:

1. ☐ Car  ☐ Truck  ☐ RV  ☐ Boat
   **Parking Required:** ☐ Garage  ☐ Carport  ☐ Driveway  ☐ Street

2. ☐ Car  ☐ Truck  ☐ RV  ☐ Boat
   **Parking Required:** ☐ Garage  ☐ Carport  ☐ Driveway  ☐ Street

3. ☐ Car  ☐ Truck  ☐ RV  ☐ Boat
   **Parking Required:** ☐ Garage  ☐ Carport  ☐ Driveway  ☐ Street

The following ADA-type accommodations (e.g., ramp, wide doorways, etc.) are preferred/required (circle one): _____

# Contractor Evaluation Checklist

Rank the contractors on a scale of 1 to 5, with 1 being poor or not applicable and 5 being excellent or strongly applicable.

| 1. Interpersonal Skills & Communication | 1 | 2 | 3 | 4 | 5 |
|---|---|---|---|---|---|
| a. Your interactions | 1 | 2 | 3 | 4 | 5 |
| b. Reports from your architect/designer | 1 | 2 | 3 | 4 | 5 |
| c. Reports from client references | 1 | 2 | 3 | 4 | 5 |

Notes/Supporting Data:_____

_____

_____

_____

_____

_____

| 2. Knowledge & Expertise | 1 | 2 | 3 | 4 | 5 |
|---|---|---|---|---|---|
| a. Provided quality input and suggestions | 1 | 2 | 3 | 4 | 5 |
| b. Pointed out potential pitfalls and delays and suggested solutions | 1 | 2 | 3 | 4 | 5 |
| c. Assessed compliance of plans with local building codes | 1 | 2 | 3 | 4 | 5 |

Notes/Supporting Data:_____

_____

_____

_____

_____

_____

3. Professionalism                                      1   2   3   4   5

   a. Clarity and thoroughness of bid, contract,    1   2   3   4   5
      and warranty

   b. Licensed                                          1   2   3   4   5

   c. Bonded (if necessary by local law or              1   2   3   4   5
      if advertised)

   d. Carries general liability and worker's            1   2   3   4   5
      compensation insurance

   e. BBB report                                        1   2   3   4   5

   f. Easy to reach by telephone and/or email       1   2   3   4   5

   Notes/Supporting Data:_____

   _____

   _____

   _____

   _____

   _____


4. Quality of work                                      1   2   3   4   5

   a. Past projects                                     1   2   3   4   5

   b. Current projects                                  1   2   3   4   5

   c. Aesthetic similar to yours                        1   2   3   4   5

   Notes/Supporting Data:_____

   _____

   _____

   _____

   _____

   _____

5. Cost      1   2   3   4   5

| | 1 | 2 | 3 | 4 | 5 |
|---|---|---|---|---|---|
| a. Similar to other bids | 1 | 2 | 3 | 4 | 5 |
| b. Much higher than other bids | 1 | 2 | 3 | 4 | 5 |
| c. Much lower than other bids | 1 | 2 | 3 | 4 | 5 |
| d. Negotiable | 1 | 2 | 3 | 4 | 5 |
| e. Firm | 1 | 2 | 3 | 4 | 5 |

Notes/Supporting Data:_____

_____

_____

_____

_____

_____

APPENDIX *B*

# Real Speak
# From Builders and
# Designers

## Budgeting for Success

*KAREN DRY*
*President, Garrett Interiors, Inc.*

A good interior design firm can help a home owner translate her vision into a more accurate bottom line on the project. Interior designers can provide expert information about what it actually takes to design and install the special features in a home and avoid construction and change orders that can considerably drive up the costs. Basically, a good interior designer speaks three languages, that of architect, contractor, and inspired home owner.

At Garrett Interiors, we've created a preconstruction review and project budget analysis to assist clients who are taking on new build or remodels. We developed this consulting service after frequently witnessing dream homes becoming nightmares because of budget constraints. Most budget problems can be avoided if the home owner is aware of all the options available prior to building. Our systematic approach has saved our clients time, money, and aggravation.

For example, we had a client who wanted to expand her kitchen to create a great room. She came to us with grand ideas. She wanted to add a previously non-existent fireplace that she'd seen at a romantic bed-and-breakfast to her new kitchen and cover it in aged brick and mahogany paneling. However, the contractor and architect had not included these materials in their initial bids. Most architects and contractors will budget for mid-level items. No architect or contractor likes to bid high, especially if the finished architectural carpentry and associated items are unique.

When we gave her an idea of what that level of design and project construction implementation would cost, it threw her budget way out of whack. So we offered her valid construction and material alternatives to meet her desired look without breaking the bank. We presented her with a final budget in a complete package that was suitable for bank and loan review.

Most customers focus on collecting bids for construction, architectural design, and main material costs. However, they seldom consider what it will cost to complete the remodel or new build, such as the furniture they need to enjoy that wood burning fireplace with a brick hearth. Typically, a homeowner needs to budget $35 to $70 per square foot for furniture, drapery, and accessories in addition to the construction and design costs.

Careful budgeting and a realistic approach to the entire process—design, construction and the actual living in the space—makes a true recipe for home construction and remodel success.

## Define Your Needs Early On

*JOANNE (JO) THEUNISSEN*
*President, Howling Hammer Builders, Inc.*

As a small-volume custom builder, I have had many wonderful experiences dealing with my female clients (and unless I build for a single man, my clients usually are women). However, I have also had more than my share of difficult clients. Difficulties seldom arise from a client's bad personality, rather problems crop up when the client has no real vision of what she wants.

Building or remodeling a home should not be approached as an impulse purchase. Many extremely intelligent women have made their builder's life (as well as their own) miserable simply because they did not consider what they truly want or expect from the construction process.

I recently took on a custom build for a client who had originally wanted to remodel an existing home. She and her husband had worked with an architect to design the project for over a year. The plans called for increasing the square footage of the existing home by 75% and actually digging out an in-ground pool to accommodate the necessary additional foundation.

In the process of discussing the specifications for kitchen and bathrooms I discovered that my client didn't like the fixture choices or the locations of appliances, and she didn't think the rooms would be functional for her family's lifestyle. Although she had spent considerable time with the architect planning to make the house look great, she had given very little consideration to how she actually lived or what she really wanted in her home. She was building a showplace, not a home. Long story short, we started over.

Luckily she owned an adjacent vacant lot that we could build new on. We designed a home based on how she and her family actually wanted to live in the space. The newly designed home resembles the original architect's plans only in its architectural style. Everything else changed—the size and location of rooms and the number of bedrooms and bathrooms. It turns out the most important room to her was the prayer/meditation room, which didn't even exist on the first plan.

If we had not taken the time to thoroughly discuss the project early on, we would have executed a plan to perfection, but we would have had a very unhappy client when the work was complete. Because of her hesitancy to discuss her own personal desires and needs with her architect, she almost ended up with a home that had been designed "for" her, not "with" her.

# Designing a Healthy Home

*MICHELLE A. ROBERTS*
*Founder of Chatham Hill Residential Design and Build, LLC and*
*founder and creator of ecohealth^sm homes by Caroline McKennasm*

As a residential designer and builder I view home construction holistically. My approach is the result of my own experiences in creating a healthy home for my family. In October 2001, my life was pretty full; I was a wife, a mother of a newborn and a toddler, and an amateur designer. My newborn daughter Caroline was severely colicky, she never slept, and her nose was constantly either runny or congested. I took her to the best pediatricians and specialists that Boston had to offer. They all diagnosed Caroline as perfectly healthy. However, my maternal instinct told me otherwise. As it turned out Caroline, now 18 months, had severe sensory integration dysfunction. I also knew she was allergic to something, the question was—what?

Because small children spend most of their lives inside, I knew I could make Caroline's quality of life better if I changed her home environment. I read everything I could find on sensory integration dysfunction and environmental allergies.

In 1998, prior to purchasing our current home, our home inspector uncovered only two issues that needed to be addressed. As a result of a spring melt, water had seeped through the basement floor cracks and the six-year-old rotted Masonite siding needed to be replaced. We fixed the problems by replacing the damaged siding and installing a $4,500 French drain, sump pump, and dehumidifier. We thought we could finally relax and enjoy our home without worries.

We started working on designing and renovating our home to fit Caroline's health needs. We replaced most of the carpets with hardwood and removed most of the window treatments throughout the house. When we pulled up the carpet we found nails, sawdust, razor blades, candy wrappers, and cigarette butts! When we demolished the bathroom to replace the sheetrock with beautiful floor-to-ceiling beadboard, we found even more garbage—soda cans, empty fast food wrappers, scraps of wood, etc.

Finally, I redesigned Caroline's bedroom, the kid's bathroom, the kitchen, and the playroom to address Caroline's sensory needs. I was able to create a calming environment for Caroline by using soothing warm colors, ambient lighting, soft pillows and bedding, and decorating with stuffed animals. I added ceiling speakers throughout the house because music also had a calming effect on Caroline. I also kept our home fresh and clean.

The design changes seemed to help her sensory issues, but she was still suffering from nasal congestion. I even developed allergy symptoms. Was our home making us sick? To make a long story short, yes, it was. Our home was poorly constructed, and we had mold issues that affected the indoor air quality. As a result, we had to do a total overhaul of our home.

It is absolutely critical to make sure you know what products, materials, and construction methods your designer-builder uses when remodeling or building a home. Also, make sure that they are cleaning thoroughly during the construction process. Today my family is healthy (and so is our home) due to sustainable-healthy building products and materials, and building science!

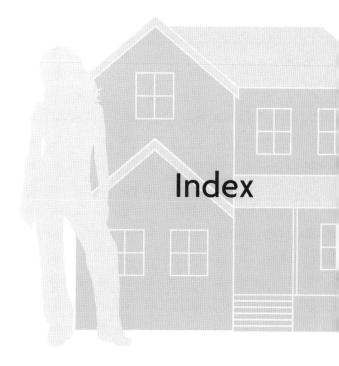

# Index

The National Association of Home Builders is a Washington-based trade association representing more than 235,000 members involved in home building, remodeling, multifamily construction, property management, trade contracting, design, housing finance, building product manufacturing, and other aspects of residential and light commercial construction. Known as "the voice of the housing industry," NAHB is affiliated with more than 800 state and local home builders associations around the country. NAHB's builder members construct about 80 percent of all new residential units, supporting one of the largest engines of economic growth in the country: housing.

 **Join the National Association of Home Builders** by joining your local home builders association. Visit www.nahb.org/join or call 800-368-5242, x0, for information on state and local associations near you. Great member benefits include:

- Access to the **National Housing Resource Center** and its collection of electronic databases, books, journals, videos, and CDs. Call 800-368-5254, x8296 or e-mail nhrc@nahb.org
- **Nation's Building News**, the weekly e-newsletter containing industry news. Visit www.nahb.org/nbn
- **Extended access to www.nahb.org** when members log in. Visit www.nahb.org/login
- **Business Management Tools** for members only that are designed to help you improve strategic planning, time management, information technology, customer service, and other ways to increase profits through effective business management. Visit www.nahb.org/biztools
- **Council membership**:
  **Building Systems Council**: www.nahb.org/buildingsystems
  **Commercial Builders Council**: www.nahb.org/commercial
  **Building Systems Council's Concrete Home Building Council**: www.nahb.org/concrete
  **Multifamily Council**: www.nahb.org/multifamily
  **National Sales & Marketing Council**: www.nahb.org/nsmc
  **Remodelors™ Council**: www.nahb.org/remodelors
  **Women's Council**: www.nahb.org/womens
  **50+ Housing Council**: www.nahb.org/50plus

 **BuilderBooks**, the book publishing arm of NAHB, publishes inspirational and educational products for the housing industry and offers a variety of books, software, brochures, and more in English and Spanish. Visit www.BuilderBooks.com or call 800-223-2665. NAHB members save at least 10% on every book.

 **BuilderBooks Digital Delivery** offers over 30 publications, forms, contracts, and checklists that are instantly delivered in electronic format to your desktop. Visit www.BuilderBooks.com and click on Digital Delivery.

 The **Member Advantage Program** offers NAHB members discounts on products and services such as computers, automobiles, payroll services, and much more. Keep more of your hard-earned revenue by cashing in on the savings today. Visit www.nahb.org/ma for a comprehensive overview of all available programs.